Amazing GRACE

Publications International, Ltd.

Let's get social!
 @Publications_International
@PublicationsInternational
www.pilbooks.com

Contents

Amazing Grace

God's amazing grace can transform our lives. When we open our hearts to God's love, we see how his blessings flow through us.

Sometimes, his grace is more difficult to see. We go through periods of doubt and anger, when God seems distant from us. We feel lost, and it becomes easier to justify our failures and sinfulness. We move further from God, sometimes with sharp defiance, sometimes with apathy. But then we see God's light shining through in some way: through nature, or the words of a friend, or an epiphany during a crisis. We experience the power of God's grace once again.

In this book, you'll find a reflection, prayer, or story of faith for each day of the year. Spending time with God daily in prayer helps us pay attention to the moments of grace in our lives. The more you look around with an open heart, the more you will see how God's grace abounds, the fulfillment of the promises he has made to you.

Amazing grace! how sweet the sound,
that saved a wretch; like me!
I once was lost, but now am found,
was blind, but now I see.

'Twas grace that taught my heart to fear,
and grace my fears relieved;
how precious did that grace appear
the hour I first believed!

The Lord hath promised good to me,
his word my hope secures;
he will my shield and portion be
as long as life endures.

When we've been there ten thousand years,
bright shining as the sun,
we've no less days to sing God's praise
than when we first begun.

January

January 1

For the Lord God is a sun and shield: the Lord will give grace and glory: no good thing will he withhold from them that walk uprightly.

—Psalm 84:11

Lord, please bless this new year! I'm already seeing my calendar fill up with obligations and social events, but I want to take time this day—and every day—to focus on you. I ask you to bless my endeavors this year, to guide me to the people you want me to have in my life and activities you have in mind for me. Let me never be so busy and frazzled that I don't see the signs of your grace around me.

January 2

For thou wilt light my candle: the Lord my God will enlighten my darkness.

—Psalm 18:28

God, your blessings abound. Even in the dark of winter, I see your hand in the beauty of frost on the windowpane, the kindness of the grocery clerk who helps an elderly woman load her purchases in her car, and the diligence of those who work at night to clear the roads. Even though it gets dark early these days, I see your light shining.

January 3

'Tis so sweet to trust in Jesus,
just to take him at his word,
just to rest upon his promise,
and to know "Thus saith the Lord."

Jesus, Jesus, how I trust him!
How I've proved him o'er and o'er!
Jesus, Jesus, precious Jesus!
O for grace to trust him more!

—Louisa M.R. Stead

January 4

Charity suffereth long, and is kind; charity envieth not; charity vaunteth not itself, is not puffed up, Doth not behave itself unseemly, seeketh not her own, is not easily provoked, thinketh no evil; Rejoiceth not in iniquity, but rejoiceth in the truth; Beareth all things, believeth all things, hopeth all things, endureth all things.

—1 Corinthians 13:4–7

Today has not been a horrible day, but it has not been a good one either. I've been snappish and irritable, having to work hard to be kind to my coworkers, patient with my children, loving to my spouse. There's no particular reason why—just one of those days. Lord, please let me act with love—with patience, with kindness, with self-control—even when I'm feeling small and petty.

January 5

I write unto you, little children, because your sins are forgiven you for his name's sake.

—*1 John 2:12*

Lord, sometimes I resist your grace. It's not that I don't want to be closer to you, but I know I don't deserve it. I stew over my past sins, wallowing in guilt. I don't want to take your forgiveness for granted, but neither do I want to forget that you are always reaching out to me, ready to draw me back to you.

January 6

The year her husband died, Margaret almost didn't put the Christmas decorations out. Her grief was still fresh, and though she had muddled through Thanksgiving, she didn't know how she could get through the Christmas season. Right before Christmas, though, she found that the empty spaces bothered her more. She cried as she put the decorations out, remembering happier times when they had done so together, but she felt better for doing so.

As she packed the decorations away, she found herself grateful—for the memories behind each ornament, for the friends who had made sure she was not alone during the season, and for God's presence during her time of grief.

January 7

Let us therefore come boldly unto the throne of grace, that we may obtain mercy, and find grace to help in time of need.

—Hebrews 4:16

No one wants a health problem with an uncertain diagnosis. No one wants to wait and go through numerous tests to see if something is serious or not. Lord, please help me through this time of need. I pray that there will be nothing to this health scare—but if there is something wrong, please grant me the grace to accept the change and stress.

January 8

Marvelous grace of our loving Lord,
grace that exceeds our sin and our guilt,
yonder on Calvary's mount outpoured,
there where the blood of the Lamb was spilt.

Grace, grace, God's grace,
grace that will pardon and cleanse within;
grace, grace, God's grace,
grace that is greater than all our sin.

—Julia Johnston

January 9

Every time I feel the Spirit moving in my heart, I will pray.

Spiritual

Tom struggled to find time for prayer. The mornings were rushed with getting the kids out the door to school. He needed to pay attention to the road during his commute to and from work, and work itself kept him busy. By the end of the day, after getting the kids to bed, he and his wife were tired and in no mood to pray. The family attended church services on Sunday, but it was hard to see God's presence throughout the week.

But then there was a scare with one of the children—Tom got a phone call that there had been a car accident while his daughter was carpooling home from a sports activity. As Tom rushed to the hospital, he prayed. When his daughter was fine, just shaken up, he thanked God. And in the days after, he made a new effort to pray throughout the day, and asked for God's grace in sustaining that effort.

God, grant us the grace to turn to you, to find opportunities for prayer throughout the day.

January 10

Train up a child in the way he should go: and when he is old, he will not depart from it.

—Proverbs 22:6

One of my kids talked back to me today, God—and you gave me the grace to handle it well! I know this is something I struggle with, teaching and allowing independence while also instilling values of respect. I've brought this to you in prayer so many times. And today it felt like that habit of prayer paid off; I took a breath and was able to be loving in my response. Thank you, Lord.

January 11

As every man hath received the gift, even so minister the same one to another, as good stewards of the manifold grace of God.

—*1 Peter 4:9–11*

One of my friends is going through a difficult time, and I don't know what to do. I feel so helpless.

You know his needs, Lord, better than I do. I hold him up to you in prayer. If there is some way you can use me to help him, I ask that you plant the idea in my head. I ask that any words I say to him be inspired by you.

January 12

When I look in my child's eyes, I see the past—the many limbs of the family tree reaching forward to meet in this unique soul.

When I look in my child's eyes, I see the present—the ability to grab each moment and squeeze out each delicious drop.

When I look in my child's eyes, I see the future—all that she will be, all that she will do.

Thank you, God.

January 13

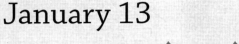

Some people say a healthy marriage is dependent on the ability of spouses to meet each other's needs. But when I think of the emotional distress and anxiety I sometimes experience, what an impossible challenge for my spouse to live up to! Our marriage is built on interdependence but, thank goodness, it is also deeply grounded in a commitment to the One who can meet both our needs.

January 14

Now the God of patience and consolation grant you to be likeminded one toward another according to Christ Jesus.

—Romans 15:5

It's not hard to love those who sparkle—the diamond people in the world. The real test of loving is being able to love those who are like pieces of coal, those diamonds in the rough who might get us dirty. But if we love them even so—with enough positive pressure from love, one day they'll be diamonds too! Lord, grant me grace in dealing with my own diamonds in the rough.

January 15

We've all heard that "actions speak louder than words." And so it is with the Christian life. Like it or not, we affect others by what we say and do. The Bible admonishes us to "Let not mercy and truth forsake thee: bind them about thy neck; write them upon the table of thine heart" (Proverbs 3:3). We are instructed to "...mercies, kindness, humbleness of mind, meekness, longsuffering" (Colossians 3:12). Whether with friends, family, coworkers, or even total strangers, we know, God, that you want us to always treat others with the utmost care and respect.

God, I can't do it alone. I ask you to extend your grace to me, that I see with your loving eyes.

January 16

Therefore take heed to your spirit, and let none deal treacherously against the wife of his youth.

—Malachi 2:15

When Polly can't feed herself, Sam bends to help her. When she falters in mid-step, lost in her own mind, he guides her steps. When she weeps in confusion, in pain, or in fear, he comforts her and in caring for her finds easing of his own pain. In sickness and in health, Sam had vowed, and now he keeps his promise. And as he ministers to her, he prays, every day, every hour, for God's grace to guide him.

January 17

But Noah found grace in the eyes of the Lord.

—Genesis 6:8

Let me set my compass to your will, Lord. Let me not be afraid to follow you, even if that pits me against the world's values. Give me a humble heart, Lord, so that I will not judge others—but please give me the gift of moral clarity as well, to seek to live by your values and do your will.

January 18

And we know that all things work together for good to them that love God, to them who are the called according to his purpose.

—Romans 8:28

How often we mourn a shattered dream, a goal not met, a vision unfulfilled. Yet amid the pieces of one shattered dream often lie the makings of an even grander design for our life. What sometimes appears as a disappointing ending is, in truth, the beginning of a whole new and exciting road ahead.

Lord, today I thank you for my disappointments.

January 19

And let us consider one another to provoke unto love and to good works: Not forsaking the assembling of ourselves together, as the manner of some is; but exhorting one another.

—Hebrews 10:24–25

The words "alone," "lonely," and "abandoned" all contain the word "one." When we believe we stand by ourselves to face life's difficulties—just one person against the world—we will often feel alone, lonely, and abandoned. But in the words "community," "fellowship," and "family," there is no longer the possibility that one might be left to stand alone.

Lord, I see you in others. Let me also carry your Word and your love to others—in my family, in my community, in my church, even to strangers.

January 20

Then Eli answered and said, Go in peace: and the God of Israel
grant thee thy petition that thou hast asked of him.
And she said, Let thine handmaid find grace in thy sight. So the
woman went her way, and did eat, and her countenance was
no more sad.

—1 Samuel 1:17–18

Lord, I know how Hannah felt. She took her struggles with infertility to you in prayer, and "poured out [her] soul" to you passionately and honestly. Witnessing her, Eli misunderstood, thinking she was drunk. But when they talked, he displayed your compassion to her and relayed a promise, and Hannah went away trusting in your promise. I am sometimes more skeptical than Hannah, Lord. Please grant me the grace to trust that my struggles are witnessed by you, and that you care for me and have the best path for me in mind.

January 21

And in that day thou shalt say, O Lord, I will praise thee: though thou wast angry with me, thine anger is turned away, and thou comfortedst me.

—Isaiah 12:1

Traumatic events leave a void in our souls that only a closer relationship with God can fill. By asking God to help us through hard times, we truly come to understand that we are never alone and that sadness is only a precursor to joy and pain a precursor to healing.

January 22

Wings of light surround me,
and I am enlightened.
Wings of love enfold me,
and I am comforted.
Angels guide my journey,
and I am directed.
Angels keep me safe from harm,
and I am protected.

Songs of joy fill me,
and I am enchanted.
Songs of love envelop me,
and I am empowered.
Angels sing above me,
and I am adored.
Angels chant in glory,
and I am restored.

January 23

Peace I leave with you, my peace I give unto you: not as the world giveth, give I unto you. Let not your heart be troubled, neither let it be afraid.

—John 14:27

Why can't I be happy? I ask myself. The answer is simply, I can! Happiness is a day-to-day choice, not a by-product of a circumstance or an event like winning the lottery or getting a big promotion. There are plenty of miserable lottery winners, and numerous corporate executives suffer from depression despite their six-figure salaries. I can't buy happiness, and no one can hand it to me. It is a choice. It comes from within, and it is always available, just waiting for me to recognize it.

Help me to see you working in my life, Lord, for that alone can give me true happiness.

January 24

At age four, my brother believed he could outrun any car because the soles of his new sandals looked like tire tread. "Watch me!" he shouted over his shoulder as he dashed down a hill at the summer camp where we were vacationing. Just then he took a nasty spill, cutting his knee and injuring his pride. As he wailed, my parents rushed over to comfort him.

How like that little boy I can be: Look, God, I'm all ready to do great things for you. I've got all the right credentials and intentions. Just watch me! Then fwomp! Down I go. But even while my wounds are stinging and my pride is still smarting, there is God comforting me, and his very presence brings me back to my senses, back to the humble dependence on him once again.

January 25

Tonight there was a shooting star—a bright arc of starlight sprinting into the darkness. I looked for a trace of it, to no avail. There was no trail against the deep dusk. No scar in the atmosphere. And as I mused at what I had seen, the "fixed fires"—the other stars—burned on.

Some people, though sweeping swiftly like a shooting star through our lives, can be a wonderful presence that stirs our imagination and awakens our sleeping sense of adventure. Other people are more like the stars that appear each night: always with us, faithful to the end. Which of these do we need the most in our experience? Perhaps the answer is both. For each has its own kind of light that infuses our life with joy and blessing.

God, thank you for the blessing of my friends.

January 26

The joy of the Lord is your strength.

—Nehemiah 8:10

If food is nourishment for the hungry body, then laughter is food for the downcast spirit in need of a lift. Only when the heart learns to lighten up, and the mind stops taking everything so seriously, can the spirit finally break free and dance for the sheer joy of it. God, thank you for the blessing of laughter.

January 27

I will greatly rejoice in the Lord, my soul shall be joyful in my God; for he hath clothed me with the garments of salvation, he hath covered me with the robe of righteousness, as a bridegroom decketh himself with ornaments, and as a bride adorneth herself with her jewels.

—*Isaiah 61:10*

The past does not have to be an enemy, Rather, let it be a friend and an ally that reminds you of where you've been, how far you've come, and what you've learned along the way. Then let it go as you would a favorite but little-used old garment, with love and gratitude, knowing that God will always provide you with something wonderful and new to wear along the way.

January 28

Surely he scorneth the scorners: but he giveth grace unto the lowly.

—Proverbs 3:34

Lord, I ask that you give me the gift of humility. Sometimes I get full of myself. I want to share my faith with a friend, and instead it turns into something close to boasting, as if I have it all figured out. Lord, you are the one who grants me the grace to walk on this path towards you. You are the one who draws me back when I stumble. My best efforts pale next to your grace.

January 29

Among the proliferation of bumper-sticker slogans, statements and sentiments, there's one sticker that encourages people to "practice random acts of kindness." It's a great little reminder. For whenever we make a conscious effort to be kind to others—especially to those whom we usually tend to avoid, overlook, or ignore—we take the first step toward seeing them as God sees them: through the eyes of love.

God, grant me the grace to see a chance today to perform a random act of kindness. And don't let me get so caught up in the idea of a "perfect" act of kindness that I miss a chance!

January 30

Whosoever therefore shall humble himself as this little child, the same is greatest in the kingdom of heaven.

—*Matthew 18:4*

So much need around us, O Lord. Inspire me to teach the children how to care for those who need. Even the smallest gesture in the hand of a child is more powerful than magic, bringing moments of peace and contentment into circumstances thought hopeless. Help me to become childlike in my care for others.

January 31

Once upon a winter's morn
before the sun dawned, dancing high,
In the hazy half-light calling
I thought I heard an angel cry,
Piercing the fog of slumber came the whisper,
hardly more than just a sigh,
Sweetly, softly, the silvery voice said,
"Awake, awake, the time is nigh!
Shake off the bands of hate and envy
and break the bonds of fear,
Each life has meaning—every one—
there are no worthless here.
Let love unfettered sweep the land,
let all contention cease,
Awake from the sleep of ignorance
and spread good news of peace."
And as the daybreak cleared
the mountains letting in the sun,
Softly as the lifting mist,
the heavenly angel's voice was gone.

February

February 1

Well, it's a new month. We're in the dregs of winter, though, and it's hard to feel fresh and new. It's been gray and dreary outside, and the kids are bored and restless, tired of school and eager for spring sports to begin again.

Lord, I know you take us where we're at. Please give me the grace to see the blessings in the ordinary and humdrum. Thank you for the crises that aren't happening, the text from a friend with a funny joke, my spouse taking the car in for an oil change. Bless my family, and my friends, and the service workers I meet as I run my errands.

February 2

I cannot show my children perfection, but I can illustrate excellence.

I cannot always give them their way, but I can demonstrate compromise.

I cannot make their path easy, but I can help them learn determination.

I cannot keep them from feeling pain, but I can teach them how to love.

I cannot force their relationship with you, Lord, but I can hold them up to you in prayer.

February 3

And now for a little space grace hath been shewed from the Lord our God, to leave us a remnant to escape, and to give us a nail in his holy place, that our God may lighten our eyes, and give us a little reviving in our bondage.

—Ezra 9:8

Chronic pain is not easy to deal with. You know, Father God, that I constantly fight discouragement, that I feel trapped by this contrary body. Please grant me a little grace today, to set my focus on others, and on you.

February 4

Gracious God, help us to learn from the children in our lives. Let us view the world with their innocent eyes and laugh joyously with them at the wonder of your creation. Make us mindful of others' hurts and sympathetic to others' needs. Open our hearts to the world, as children open themselves, with delight and curiosity, to all the world's experiences.

February 5

A friend loveth at all times, and a brother is born for adversity.

—Proverbs 17:17

Thank you, God, for those in my life who are like family...the childhood friend who has become a sister of the heart, the college friend who has been an honorary uncle to the kids, the neighbor who dispenses grandfatherly wisdom. Thank you for the blessing of love. Let me, too, open my heart to others.

February 6

Lord, remind us of a childhood memory of someone in uniform who made a difference in our lives. A school nurse who comforted us, a firefighter who spoke to us on a field trip to the local station, a police officer standing on the neighborhood corner, a doctor who treated us for a childhood illness. Thank you for showing us that someone in uniform could be trusted and could be a friend.

February 7

Be not forgetful to entertain strangers: for thereby some have entertained angels unawares.

—Hebrews 13:2

In this day and age, angels are more likely to appear in street clothes than in long white robes and haloes. A neighbor who offers sound advice, a mentor who shows us how to live well, a friend who comforts us—they can all act as angels. If we live open to the possibility that God will use those around us to guide our way, then we may benefit from the guidance our earthly angels give. We may not hear harps playing or get goose bumps at the time, but in hindsight we may give thanks for God's angels on earth.

February 8

Provoke not your children to wrath: but bring them up in the nurture and admonition of the Lord.

—Ephesians 6:4

I feel your hand on mine as I learn to be a good parent, O God, knowing that together you and I are instilling lifelong values and beliefs. I wish it were a straight-lined experience, but for me, it is more like a zigzag, making my growth seem slow. And yet, I am grateful for all the help you give.

February 9

Come now, and let us reason together, saith the Lord: though your sins be as scarlet, they shall be as white as snow; though they be red like crimson, they shall be as wool.

—Isaiah 1:18

When it seems that scarcely a day ends by saying, "If only I could do it over. I regret what I said, did, or didn't do," the God of fresh starts is eager to make things right. All you need to say is, "Forgive me for today, and show me how to redeem myself for tomorrow." Amazing grace, indeed.

February 10

I know not why God's wondrous grace
to me he has made known,
nor why, unworthy, Christ in love
redeemed me for his own.

But "I know whom I have believed,
and am persuaded that he is able
to keep that which I've committed
unto him against that day."

I know not how this saving faith
to me he did impart,
nor how believing in his Word
wrought peace within my heart.

But "I know whom I have believed,
and am persuaded that he is able
to keep that which I've committed
unto him against that day."

—D. W. Whittle

February 11

Remember the days of old, consider the years of many generations: ask thy father, and he will shew thee; thy elders, and they will tell thee.

—Deuteronomy 32:7

As I've grown older, I've learned to appreciate my grandmother. I love her sense of humor, her endless stories about "the way things used to be," and the wealth of knowledge that she gained from the passage of time and the overcoming of trials. I value the time I'd had to get to know her. Her connection with the past is priceless.

February 12

Behold, how good and how pleasant it is for brethren to dwell together in unity!

—Psalm 133:1

Opposites don't attract nearly as often as they repel, if we are to believe the headlines. Pick a race, color, creed, or lifestyle, Lord of all, and we'll find something to fight about. Deliver us from stereotypes. Inspire us to spot value in everyone we meet. As we dodge the curses and hatred, we are relieved there is room for all of us beneath your wings. Bless our diversity; may it flourish.

February 13

Defend the poor and fatherless: do justice to the afflicted and needy.

—Psalm 82:3

Life's not fair, and I stomp my foot in frustration. The powerful get more so as the rest of us shrink, dreams for peace are shattered as bullies get the upper hand, and despair is a tempting pit to fall into. Help me hold on, for you are a God of justice and dreams, of turning life upside down. Let me help; thanks for listening in the meantime.

February 14

Beloved, let us love one another: for love is of God; and every one that loveth is born of God, and knoweth God. He that loveth not knoweth not God; for God is love.

—*1 John 4:7–8*

It's Valentine's Day! While this holiday can be commercial, let me take it as an opportunity to thank you, God, for the people I love and the people who love me. I know all love ultimately flows from you, for you are love.

February 15

The Lord by wisdom hath founded the earth; by understanding hath he established the heavens. By his knowledge the depths are broken up, and the clouds drop down the dew.

My son, let not them depart from thine eyes: keep sound wisdom and discretion: So shall they be life unto thy soul, and grace to thy neck. Then shalt thou walk in thy way safely, and thy foot shall not stumble. When thou liest down, thou shalt not be afraid: yea, thou shalt lie down, and thy sleep shall be sweet.

—Proverbs 3:19–24

Lord, you know the worries that keep me awake some nights. Please deliver me from this fretfulness, and grant me a deep and true trust in you and your wisdom.

February 16

Wherefore, my beloved brethren, let every man be swift to hear, slow to speak, slow to wrath: For the wrath of man worketh not the righteousness of God.

—James 1:19–20

We are living in times when mouths are open, tongues are flapping, and we are quick to talk, giving sound bites of advice rather than truly listening to others. The result is that we share neither wisdom nor understanding, and those we treasure the most are left feeling alone and unheard.

February 17

Ye have received the Spirit of adoption, whereby we cry, Abba, Father.
—Romans 8:15

Despite tiredness and worry, I have moments of sheer, cartwheeling, rainbow-dancing pride and joy. I hope there are times when you say that of me. Maybe today, as I join my kids to play in the leaves, make snow angels, pack a picnic, learn the latest dance move, share pizza, or just celebrate being together. Take our hands, and jump with us for joy!

February 18

Iron sharpeneth iron; so a man sharpeneth the countenance of his friend.

—Proverbs 27:17

We are big on heroes, God. Every area of our lives has a favorite except perhaps the most important: our faith. An Aquinas or Augustine can't hold a candle to the Hollywood celebrities of our day. How sad we willingly settle for superficiality rather than substance. Help us desire being grounded as well as entertained.

February 19

If I'm grumpy…you sit beside me with your arms crossed, too.
If I'm sad…you share my tears.
If I need comfort…you open your arms.
If I'm ecstatic and want to yell it from the mountains…you echo my voice across the valley.
That's what I'm most thankful for. I never have to explain myself—I just have to be me.

February 20

When a relationship is not working—a friendship, a family tie, even a marriage—it can come to the question: should I go or stay? Unrealized dreams litter my path and the future—alone—looks better than the past— together. Is this temporary boredom and strife or permanent trouble? Facing this reality is the first step in healing; your grace is promise enough to keep going until I know.

February 21

Trust in the Lord with all thine heart; and lean not unto thine
own understanding. In all thy ways acknowledge him, and he
shall direct thy paths.

—Proverbs 3:5–6

I can do it myself, I protest, but, O God, I know it's not true. Open
me to your limitless love found in the skillful caring of those
who know firsthand my present trouble. They bring your message
home and I feel you close, as close as angel wings beating gently
upon my stubborn loneliness.

February 22

You have the power, Lord, to heal me.
I don't doubt that for a minute.
You crafted me; you can re-create me.
I trust in your creative ability.
I know you love me.
You sent your beloved Son for my redemption
and you shower me with blessings daily.
I trust in your love, Lord,
your desire to bring me health.
It's a little harder to trust in your wisdom.
I think I know what I want here.
I know what my healing will look like, sort of.
But how do you want to pull that off?
Seriously, what's your idea of my wholeness?
How would you like to accomplish my healing?
I'm guessing you'll want to touch my mind, my soul,
my attitude, my relationships, and—oh, yes—my health.
So let's do it, Lord.
I trust in your wisdom to heal all of me.
Amen.

February 23

Thy word is a lamp unto my feet, and a light unto my path.

—*Psalm 119:105*

May I rejoice in the written Word. The scriptures can come alive for me, if I only take, and read. Let me discover the acts of God in history. Travel with his disciples along the pathway of service. See how his church began, how it grew down through the centuries. Yes, let me celebrate the written Word, for it is a mirror of, and a witness to, the Living Word of the heavens.

February 24

When you're stuck on the ground,
friends help you fly.
When you give up,
friends tell you to try.
When all is dark,
friends show you the light.
When you stray from your path,
friends set you right.
Life has its ups and downs, it's true,
but friends will always be there for you.
Thank you, God, for the grace of friends,
your love through them that never ends.

February 25

Square by square, we live our lives marked off in neat appointment-calendar blocks of time. Everybody gets only so much, no more, for the lines are already bulging. We pencil in commitments that spill over into tomorrow's squares. And just look at yesterday's notations: Nowhere did we get every "to do" done, every deadline met. There is not enough time in the little squares we have allotted ourselves, O God, calling them life. We try using a larger calendar with bigger squares, but all we do is schedule heavier. Our pencils eat up our best intentions for accepting your promised abundant life. Help us, for we want to be more than just the sum of all we had scheduled, minus what we got done, multiplied by what we wished we'd been doing, tallying up to a bottom line of regret. Guide us as we erase what is not essential. Forgive us for the day-squares where we've inched you out; their hectic dreariness reflects your absence.

February 26

Think not that I am come to send peace on earth: I came not to send peace, but a sword.

—*Matthew 10:33–34*

Lord, I have a difficult decision ahead of me. Deep down, I know what the best and most righteous course of action is. But I'm letting myself second-guess myself, pointing out that other reasonable, well-meaning people are choosing the easier path and are able to justify it to themselves.

I find myself hoping that outside circumstances will change before I have to commit to the right course of action and alienate some friends. I wonder why I have to be the one to summon up the courage to do right.

Please grant me that courage.

February 27

The mighty God, even the Lord, hath spoken, and called the earth from the rising of the sun unto the going down thereof.

—Psalm 50:1

Slowly but surely, the days are getting longer again. I'm impatient for spring to arrive. But before it does...I thank you for the blessings of the winter, God. The holidays, the snow days, the celebration of your birth. I thank you for warm clothes and hot chocolate, and the days the car started despite the chill. I thank you even for bare tree branches and gray slush!

And as the days get longer, let me appreciate the extra sunlight as a gift, a daily grace that reminds me of your love.

February 28

For if ye forgive men their trespasses, your heavenly Father
will also forgive you.

—Matthew 6:14

We know that revenge will settle nothing at this point.
It will only leave us with an emptier feeling than before.
Heal the pain in our hurts over this injustice, and somehow, as
impossible as it now seems, bring us to the place of blessing our
enemies and extending the one thing that keeps saving our
own lives: your forgiveness.

February 29

Lord, thank you for this Leap Day! Let me treat this not just as any other day, but as a special gift, a chance to turn to anew. I ask that you open my eyes today to all the instances of grace around me. Let me take a special delight in the splendor of your creation. Let me see the best in people today. Let me see even the people who get my back up with your eyes, the eyes of love.

March

March 1

And Jesus being full of the Holy Ghost returned from Jordan, and was led by the Spirit into the wilderness.

—Luke 4:1

Thank you, God, for this new month. This month brings the first inklings of spring to my area, though the trees are still bare. But that seems appropriate, during this month that takes place during the season of Lent. Lord, this month, empty my heart of distractions. Walk with me to the desert and stay with me there, as you pare away those things that draw me away from you.

March 2

For I desired mercy, and not sacrifice; and the knowledge of God more than burnt offerings.

—Hosea 6:6

Lent is traditionally a time of fasting. Lord, what do I need to fast from? Is it food, or is there something else from which I need to refrain? Gossip at church, an old and stale anger at a coworker, a habit of complaining, frustration at other drivers during my morning commute...what do I need to empty out of my life so that I can focus on you?

March 3

Now also when I am old and greyheaded, O God, forsake me not; until I have shewed thy strength unto this generation, and thy power to every one that is to come.

—*Psalm 71:18*

Thank you for the gift of ancestral faith. May I, as I take my place in the family portrait as the next generation, continue to keep you, everlasting God, as the centerpiece of our family, for your love is as ageless and steadfast as the wind calling my name. Watch over the grandchildren as you have over me in your special ways. Listen as I call out their names in echoes of those family prayers shared on my behalf through a lifetime of faith-full love.

March 4

Thus saith the Lord, The people which were left of the sword found grace in the wilderness; even Israel, when I went to cause him to rest. The Lord hath appeared of old unto me, saying, Yea, I have loved thee with an everlasting love: therefore with lovingkindness have I drawn thee.

—Jeremiah 1:2–3

Lord, as we move through this Lenten season, let me not be afraid of the wilderness. Let me not be afraid of unanswered questions, of uncertain paths, of scarcity. Let me trust in your and your loving-kindness, that I will have what I need when I need it. Let me trust in your "daily bread," and not get wound up in worries about the future.

.

March 5

After making plans to go hiking with friends, I remembered my boots were a half size too small. My budget, however, was telling me that new footwear was out of the question. Without much hope, I decided to visit a sporting-goods store. As I drove there, I spotted a thrift store and felt a strong impulse to stop in. "God, please let there be a good pair of hiking boots in my size here," I prayed. Scanning the rows of shoes, I found only one pair of authentic hiking boots, and they were in new condition. But would they fit? I fumbled to find the sizing information. When I read it, I wanted to let out a whoop, but instead I whispered, "Thank you, God!" Then, handing the cashier a mere eight dollars and some change, I couldn't help but say "Thank you" again.

March 6

And now, brethren, I commend you to God, and to the word of his grace, which is able to build you up, and to give you an inheritance among all them which are sanctified.

—*Acts 20:32*

Lord, I ask for insight when I read the Bible. Let me not dismiss those passages I don't understand, or that I find difficult. Let your words transform me from within and build me up, drawing me more deeply into connection with you.

March 7

*I am grateful, O God, that your standards run more
to how we're loving you and one another than how we
appear. If you judged on lawns, I would be
out in the cold!*

Mine is the yard where kids gather.

*Ball games, sprinkler tag's muddy marathons, snow
fort and tree house constructions, car tinkerings and
bike repair—they all happen here.*

*Bless my rutted, littered lawn, wise Creator. It's the
most beautiful landscape, dotted as it is with children
who will be grown and gone faster
than we can say "replant."*

March 8

The surge of adrenaline as we look over our shoulders to see who's gaining on us is as natural as breathing, Lord, and we pick up the pace to keep ahead. If behind, we dig in to overtake whoever is ahead of us. Competition is exhilarating, and we welcome its challenges. Yet, competition out of control creates bare-knuckle conflict within us, and we are shocked at the lengths to which we will go to win.

Help us weigh the risks and benefits of getting a corner office, promotion, and raise. Keep us achieving, Lord, for being the best, brightest, and boldest is a worthy goal. Help us win fair and square and not cheat ourselves. Help us remember that we can best gain the competitive edge by focusing on your guidance. And how, really, can we see where you are leading if we are walking backward on the lookout for whoever might be overtaking us! That is losing, no matter what we win.

March 9

I will praise thee; for I am fearfully and wonderfully made: marvellous are thy works; and that my soul knoweth right well.

—Psalm 139:14

Running is so good. Can muscles silently praise you? I catch a vision of life's goodness in the pounding of my feet, even in the sweat pouring down. You made this warm machine, and you gave me the responsibility to keep it going. I will pray now, with energy, exertion—gutting it out. But I will not pray with words for awhile. For you are here as I pick up speed. And what, after all, needs to be said aloud at this moment?

March 10

To the Lord our God belong mercies and forgivenesses, though we have rebelled against him.

—Daniel 9:9

My anger is all consuming and my fantasies are flamed by satisfying thoughts of revenge. Then, like a rustle of wind across a wheat field, I hear you reminding me that healing from violence is an issue of ecology. Is seeking revenge putting my time and energy to good use? Dear Lord, I am down on my knees with this one: Shall I rebuild or retaliate?

March 11

A banker is now a nurse, moving at mid-career from being
counter to contributor. O God, how we envy those
who take the risk.

Nudge us to get going; prod us past this middle, which like
a seat-sprung rocking chair has lulled us into settling for
being counters when we could be contributors.
Help us learn to tell the difference, for there may be ways
to modify where we are.

With your energetic belief in us, Lord, we know there is no
better time than mid-career and mid-life to change course.
Middlers have "double vision," seeing both behind and
ahead, and the view is exciting. With your help, we see that
the glass is more than half full for those who say, "I know
where I've been, and the future looks better than the past,"
and then make a new day happen.

Mid-career, mid-life, is as good a time as any to make a
change, Lord, and certainly better than never.

March 12

What a day. When all else fails, rearrange the furniture. Lend a shoulder, God of change, as I scoot the couch to a new spot. Like wanderers to your promised land, I need a fresh perspective. My life has turned topsy-turvy, and I need a new place to sit... first with you, then the rest of my world of family, friends, job. I need to be prepared for whatever happens next, and nothing says it like a redone room. I smile as I take my new seat; this is a better view.

March 13

But by the grace of God I am what I am: and his grace which was bestowed upon me was not in vain; but I laboured more abundantly than they all: yet not I, but the grace of God which was with me.

—1 Corinthians 15:18

Sometimes I take pride in my faith. I favorably compare my church involvement to that of others; I share a helpful spiritual practice with a friend not with humility but with an air of condescension. Lord, keep my gentle and humble of heart, aware of how reliant I am on you.

March 14

Preserve me, O God: for in thee do I put my trust.

—*Psalm 16:1*

You're bringing change to my life, Lord. May my nerves hold out in this transition! It's hectic making big changes. It takes away the security, the comfort, the sense of stability. We were made for change, but we prefer the status quo. We even begin to assume that where we make our home can be heaven itself. But there is only one true heaven.

March 15

Bless the nannies, sitters, and caregivers who tend our work-a-bye children, Lord, for we leave our greatest treasures in their hands. How difficult it is to drop them off on our way to work beyond home.

Sometimes we feel defensive and guilty under the stares of others who judge our working choices. But we don't make them lightly, and we do our best to ease transitions and soothe tears—both the children's and ours—in the partings. Continue to help us choose wisely; soften criticisms, both those of others and our own.

For whether we are at home all day or not, we are all full-time parents, Lord, worrying, praying, holding our young in thought twenty-four hours a day even if we cannot be by their sides every moment.

So help us, Lord, both the working-away and the staying-put parents, to fully be involved in our children's journeys through our homes, no matter on which side of the front door we spend most of it.

March 16

You said we should, "Forgive us our sins as we forgive those who sin against us." Do you realize how hard that can be?

When I've been hurt, my anger and resentment feels justified. Yet I know that my lack of forgiveness hurts me as much as it hurts the one who hurt me. I need your help with forgiveness.

Help me forgive anyone who has ever wounded me, however slight or great the hurt. Forgive me both the offenses I did on purpose and the ways I hurt others without realizing it. Whenever possible, let me know how to make amends to those I have hurt.

Help me accept forgiveness from others and graciously offer my own forgiveness. From now on, guide me in a way of living that respects other people and seeks to understand rather than to condemn their actions.

For this is the way that leads to life. Amen.

March 17

But speak thou the things which become sound doctrine: That the aged men be sober, grave, temperate, sound in faith, in charity, in patience.

—Titus 2:1–3

Today I ask you to bless those older than me. Keep their minds sharp and their bodies vigorous. Let those who have caregivers be treated kindly, with patience and respect. Let those around them listen, appreciating their hard-earned wisdom.

March 18

Lord, I've stood by too many deathbeds to ever doubt that the adage "you can't take it with you" is absolutely true. We come into this world with nothing, and we leave with nothing. So why is it so tempting to spend so much of our lifetimes striving for more money and possessions? We forget that all those things are fleeting, and that the only people who are impressed by what we accumulate are those whose values are worldly. But you, O God, are eternal! Thank you for providing a way for us to be with you forever.

March 19

I will praise thee, O Lord, with my whole heart; I will shew forth all thy marvellous works.

—Psalm 9:1

Lord, just when I was thinking I was too pooped to get through the day, I heard a praise song on the radio. It reminded me of the unending supply of energy and strength that is ours through faith in you! Thanks for getting me through the day today, Lord. I would be so lost without you.

March 20

The Lord is my shepherd; I shall not want.

—*Psalm 23:1*

Lord, how grateful we are for the rest you bring to even the most harried souls. The young soldier on the battlefield knows that peace, and so does the young mother with many mouths to feed but too little money in her bank account. You are the one who brings us to the place of restoration in our hearts and minds, Lord. Thank you for being our shepherd.

March 21

Be still, and know that I am God.

—Psalm 46:10

Easter is coming soon. Part of me wants to skip ahead to the joy of that season, as I plan for the family gathering and shop for an outfit.

But we are not quite there, yet, so let me rest in stillness with you for a while yet. Let me take time to reflect each day, even if those reflections on repentance are not always comfortable.

March 22

But if we walk in the light, as he is in the light, we have fellowship one with another, and the blood of Jesus Christ his Son cleanseth us from all sin.

—1 John 1:7

Lord, there's that joy-filled song "Walkin' on Sunshine" that comes to mind when I read this verse. And for me, the happiness of being in the light with you, the delight of walking with you, and the ongoing fellowship with my brothers and sisters in you— all this knowing that you've washed my sins away—walkin' on sunshine is just what it feels like. Thank you for calling me into your light!

March 23

Therefore if any man be in Christ, he is a new creature: old things are passed away; behold, all things are become new.

—2 Corinthians 5:17

Lord, sometimes I think back to who I was before I knew you, and I don't even recognize myself. That's how great the change is when you make us new creations! I'm so glad that the person I was isn't nearly as important in your eyes as the person you know I can be. I may have been younger and fitter then, but I was lost on this worldly adventure. Thank you, Lord, for claiming me as your own and making everything new in my life!

March 24

I exhort therefore, that, first of all, supplications, prayers, intercessions, and giving of thanks, be made for all men; For kings, and for all that are in authority; that we may lead a quiet and peaceable life in all godliness and honesty.

—1 Timothy 2:1–2

Whether we keep an actual prayer list, a list in our heads, or no list at all, it is good to keep others in our prayers. We have the privilege of being able to pray for our family members, and what a relief it is to be able to entrust them to God's care when we feel disheartened or overwhelmed. The above passage reminds us to pray also for "all who are in high positions," which could include anyone from world leaders to our boss. Jesus even told us to pray for our enemies! There isn't a soul on the face of the earth who doesn't need prayer, who doesn't need God's intervention in their lives. And who knows? Perhaps someone is praying for you, too— right at this very moment.

March 25

*The Lord is merciful and gracious, slow to anger, and
plenteous in mercy.*

—*Psalm 103:8*

Why do some see you as an angry God, eager to squash us when
we sin? Could it be that you've been misrepresented by some who
have claimed to represent you? Perhaps. But maybe at times I
myself have clung to such wrong notions about you when others
have offended me. I paint you with a human brush with such
thoughts as, if I were in God's shoes, dealing with that jerk, I'd
let that person have it. But when I gather myself, I realize you see
each of us as the beautiful being you intended; our failings may
bring you sadness, but not hatred. Your perfection is made up not
only of absolute holiness, but also of deep mercy. And how I need
that mercy every day!

March 26

Incline my heart unto thy testimonies, and not to covetousness.

—*Psalm 119:36*

Father, you've shown me that coveting isn't always as straightforward as wishing I had someone else's house or car. The covetous corruption that creeps in can wear any number of disguises, such as begrudging the fact that someone has been blessed in some way that I haven't. It can be despising someone else's success or hoping for their failure so I won't feel left behind. The list goes on, but the essence is my discontent with my own lot in life as I compare myself with someone else. Set me free today to enjoy the blessings you've provided without spoiling them by pointless comparisons.

March 27

I, even I, am he that blotteth out thy transgressions for mine own sake, and will not remember thy sins.

—Isaiah 43:25

Lord, sometimes my past rises up to haunt me—or worse yet, to bite me. These are the real-world consequences of poor choices I've made. But even though I'm reminded of them because of the cause-and-effect nature of things, once I confess them to you and receive your forgiveness, they are erased from your record book. So even when I'm reminded of my old sins in one way or another, help me to quickly let go of any guilt or shame that rears its ugly head. While consequences may linger, your forgiveness is complete. Thank you for that eternal reality.

March 28

For as many as are led by the Spirit of God, they are the sons of God.

—*Romans 8:14*

One sentiment I hear from time to time is "...after all, we're all God's children." It's usually uttered during trying times, to remind us to hold on and keep the faith. It's a comforting thought, but the verse here stresses that God's children are led by his Spirit. May we strive each day to be active children of God, praying and following the call of his Spirit rather than our own impulses and desires.

March 29

Every day I'm exposed to a world whose values don't jibe with yours, Lord. I am in need of constant reminders to not get caught up in notions that money, power, status, and physical appearance are of utmost importance. While the movers and shakers of society endorse such things as necessary for a fulfilling existence, you say that faithfulness to you is where real life is lived out and lasting inner peace is achieved. O Lord, help me when I'm tempted to believe that I can prevail in life by being seen as "strong" in ways that ultimately don't matter to you.

March 30

Lord, today I pray for all struggling parents. Give them strength to hold fast to what they know is right even in the face of conflicting opinions and advice that is well meaning but off the mark nonetheless. You alone can supply the peace of mind they need to get through the toughest of times. Stay close to them, Lord, and amaze them with your works!

March 31

Many people commonly object to churchgoing, saying, "I don't need to go to church to be near God." It's true: One can be close to God without attending service. In fact, on the other side of the coin, some folks who go to church regularly live very "worldly" lives.

So what good is church? Church is good for God, for us, and for those around us. Gathering together reminds us of our need for God and satisfies God's need of a place in our harried lives. In addition, sometimes it is good for us to be there because others are in need of our presence and support. Simply put, church is not always about our needs. It is also about what God needs and what our neighbors need. Church creates a place for all of these needs to be met.

April

April 1

My voice shalt thou hear in the morning, O Lord; in the morning will I direct my prayer unto thee, and will look up.

—Psalm 5:3

How good it is to talk to God! Formal prayer is important, but today I just want to pour out my heart and speak to God in my own words. Thank you for the opportunity to talk to you as a friend. Thank you for listening to my prayers and understanding my heart.

April 2

When her teen daughter, Joanna, was going through a rough time and feeling insecure, her mother Tiffany had some advice: to spend some time volunteering and being kind to others. Doing good, she said, had benefits both for those whom Joanna helped and for Joanna herself. "Sometimes we need to get out of our heads," she said, "and set our worries aside. Sometimes we find Christ when we're trying to be a Christ-bearer to others."

April 3

And of his fulness have all we received, and grace for grace. For the law was given by Moses, but grace and truth came by Jesus Christ.

—John 1:16–17

Jesus, I ask you to please keep drawing me into closer relationship with you. Sometimes I think of my good acts like a running tally: letting someone go ahead of me in traffic gets me a point, donating money to someone in need gets me ten. But that's a small, legalistic way of thinking. Let me do good things not in hope of a reward but simply to pass along the tremendous grace you have granted to me.

April 4

The earth is the Lord's, and the fulness thereof; the world, and they that dwell therein.

—Psalm 24:1

The trees are just beginning to bud, and my neighbor's daffodils are brightening the view. Thank you for spring, God, for new beginnings. I marvel in the beauty of your creation, the intricacies of your designs. I ask that you keep my eyes open to the wonders of nature.

April 5

Confess your faults one to another, and pray one for another, that
ye may be healed. The effectual fervent prayer of a righteous
man availeth much.

—James 5:16

Who shall I pray for today, Lord? I don't want to pray only for
my needs and my wants, but to hold others up to you in prayer.
Please bring to my mind the names of those who most need
prayer today.

April 6

Behold, I stand at the door, and knock: if any man hear my voice, and open the door, I will come in to him, and will sup with him, and he with me.

—Revelation 3:20

An open door is an invitation. Just as the gates of Heaven are open to all who follows God's will, an open door invites me in to experience new joys and revelations. Thank you, God, for allowing me to see the open doors in my life and take advantage of new experiences. Let me walk through them with Jesus at my side.

April 7

Father God, disappointments come to us all, but it is particularly poignant when my children face disappointments. I ache for them; yet there is seldom anything I can do except comfort them.

You give comfort, too, Lord. Your love has been my shield against the world's harsh realities. When I am not able to comfort my children and protect them from disappointment, help them find their comfort in you. And may we all learn to pass along to others that same comfort you have given us.

April 8

Lord, make me a model of your love, a fitting example from which those I meet can see how to live. Help me to keep my thoughts and words pure, always pleasing in your sight.

In a world where deception is commonplace, fill me with truth and honesty so I may avoid making empty promises and sending conflicting signals. May my actions always model the message of my words.

Grant me your patience and understanding so that I may listen with my heart to those in need.

Teach me to control my temper so I may provide for those I meet peace of mind rather than "a piece of my mind."

Season me with gentleness, kindness, and forgiveness so my family can experience through me the joy and richness of life with you.

April 9

God with me lying down,
God with me rising up,
God with me in each ray of light
nor I a ray of joy without him,
nor one ray without him.

Christ with me sleeping,
Christ with me waking,
Christ with me watching,
every day and night,
each day and night.
God with me protecting,
The Lord with me directing,
The Spirit with me strengthening,
forever and for evermore,
ever and evermore,
Amen.

—*Celtic Prayer*

April 10

We all prefer to deal with honest people—people we can trust—people who will not lie or try to deceive us. A noble goal for one's life is to pursue honesty—honesty with others, with ourselves, and with God. Yet it is not natural to tell the truth. Honesty can seem to leave us open to attack—to tear down the walls of protection we would rather erect in our lives. Scripture tells us, "The truth shall make you free." Although it might be hard to be honest, if we do it with loving intentions, the burden that dishonesty brings will be lifted.

April 11

For by grace are ye saved through faith; and that not of yourselves: it is the gift of God: Not of works, lest any man should boast.

—Ephesians 2:8–9

Father God, you gave a staggering gift through your son, Jesus Christ. How can I express my gratitude for the gift of salvation? Sometimes I need to sit in silence, surrounded by your presence, as I reflect on your love for me.

April 12

O God of justice, we confess that we are too quick at times to judge those around us, basing our opinions not upon what is written in their hearts but what is easily seen by our lazy eyes. Keep us faithful to challenge one another any time we find ourselves speaking in generalities about any group of people or repeating jokes and slurs that offend and degrade. Remind us that all of creation bears the imprint of your face, all people are children of yours, all souls are illuminated by your divine spark. We know that whatever diminishes others diminishes your spirit at work in them. Make us respectful, humble, and open to the diversity around us that reflects your divine imagination and creativity.

April 13

Now when he was in Jerusalem at the passover, in the feast day, many believed in his name, when they saw the miracles which he did.

—*John 2:23*

Today I will think about the miracles in my life. I am thankful that God gives me these special gifts. Miracles remind me that God is always in my life. Thank you, Lord, for showing me your power and surprising me with these moments of grace. Help me see your hand at work and trust that your way is the best.

April 14

My son, eat thou honey, because it is good; and the honeycomb, which is sweet to thy taste.

—Proverbs 24:13

How grateful I am for the sweet things I eat! Of course, I don't want to overindulge, but I get so much enjoyment out of the sweet taste! Thank you, God, for creating sweet foods. Help me enjoy them in moderation and always praise you for the sweetness in my life.

April 15

But godliness with contentment is great gain. For we brought nothing into this world, and it is certain we can carry nothing out. And having food and raiment let us be therewith content.

—1 Timothy 6:6–8

Content with just food and clothing? Really, Lord? I'm thankful that you provide for my basic needs, but there's much, much more on my wish list. This passage makes me realize how much I expect in life. Sometimes I act like I'm entitled to certain things: a well-paying job for little effort on my part, minimal traffic on the way to said job, restaurant lunches every day, seamless relationships with loved ones. Help me to be thankful for the countless blessings in my life and to always be ready to help others rather than focusing on adding to my own stores. Please guide me, Lord. I'm ready to answer your call to contentment.

April 16

When life's winds toss me
upon the waves of uncertainty and doubt,
and when the tempest beats me
and rocks of guilt and self-pity,
when my pitiful heart yearns
for love I cannot find,
when the darkness seems darker
and the night longer,
some unseen hand reaches down,
and with a strength and tenderness
I cannot comprehend,
pulls me back into the light.

April 17

Blessed is he whose transgression is forgiven, whose sin is covered.

—*Psalm 32:1*

Dear God, I know that I have wronged others over the course
of the years. I pray that those moments are long forgotten, and
if they are not, I pray that I might somehow make them right.
I truly forgive anyone who has wronged me, letting go of any
grudges or hurtful feelings. And I pray that as I forgive, so may I
be forgiven. Amen.

April 18

Lord, I wish to live a long life, but I fear growing old. I want to accomplish great things, but I fear risking what I already have. I desire to love with all my heart, but the prospect of self-revelation makes me shrink back. Perhaps for just this day, you will give me the grace that would help me reach out? Let me bypass these dreads and see instead your hand reaching back to mine—right now—just as it always has.

April 19

We are far too easily pleased, Lord. We run after our toys with such vigor. We pursue every form of recreation, as if it could somehow save us. We involve ourselves in relationship after relationship, hoping that each new conquest will give us full satisfaction. We work and work, earning more and more money, thinking that somehow happiness can be bought, or that the joy of the future can be mortgaged today.

We multiply the objects of our amusement and the means of our entertainment, believing that if we can only turn off our minds for a few hours, our true situation will disappear into the background.

Yes, we are far too easily pleased with all we can do for ourselves. But how much energy would we exert toward obtaining our true Home if we could only see the place you've prepared for us? Give us that vision, God, and the determination to reach for your promises every day.

April 20

And the child grew, and waxed strong in spirit, filled with wisdom: and the grace of God was upon him.

—Luke 2:40

Jesus, we think of you as an adult, in your public ministry. But you went through everything that we went through, all the small joys and miseries of childhood. I ask your blessing today on those children I know, that they too will grow strong in spirit and wisdom.

April 21

Thank you for the difficult people in my life. They show me that not everything can be easy. When I try to connect with someone who is hard to get along with or who doesn't agree with me, I think of how Jesus reached out even to those who did not agree with him. Allow me to be like Jesus and be thankful for the opportunity to extend my heart to everyone.

April 22

And it came to pass, as he sat at meat with them, he took bread, and blessed it, and brake, and gave to them. And their eyes were opened, and they knew him; and he vanished out of their sight.

—Luke 24:30–31

In this Easter season, I read the stories set after your resurrection...the discovery of the empty tomb, the realization along the road to Emmaus. For the early believers, this joyous time was full of uncertainty. When I am going through uncertainty, let me trust in the joy to come—that I too might find you walking next to me in the guise of a stranger.

April 23

*His mother saith unto the servants, Whatsoever he saith
unto you, do it.*

—John 2:5

Jesus fulfilled many roles during his earthly life: son, friend,
teacher, and savior. He grappled with many issues—just as we
do—but he patiently fulfilled the mission he came to earth to
perform. When family friends ran out of wine at the wedding at
Cana, Jesus' mother asked him to do something. Jesus hesitated
for a moment because he wasn't sure it was time for him to draw
such attention to himself, but he soon acquiesced, realizing that
his time had, indeed, come. May we follow Jesus' example and
always be open to your plans for our lives, Lord.

April 24

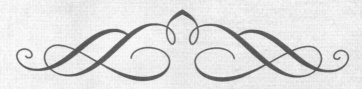

Dear God,

*It's been difficult lately. One challenge after another, one
obstacle after the next. But I know everything is for my
greatest growth and to teach me valuable lessons, and for that
I come to you today to give thanks and praise. I may get angry
and frustrated when life gets derailed, but I know in my heart
you are never giving me more than I can handle, and that
there is a blessing on the other side of each lesson you provide
me with. Those blessings are what keep me going, even on the
most troubling of days. Thank you for caring about me enough
to push me and motivate me to grow, to become a stronger,
better person through my trials and tribulations.*

I truly am blessed. Amen.

April 25

Then I will give you rain in due season, and the land shall yield her increase, and the trees of the field shall yield their fruit.

—Leviticus 26:4

Thank you for rain! Not only do April showers bring May flowers, as the old saying goes, but rain can be beautiful in its own right. Thank you for gray days and the sound of rain on the rooftop. Thank you when the basement stays dry. Thank you even when a sports event or outdoor party is canceled—when we let those things happen with calm and acceptance, we find out that your plans for us are better than our own.

April 26

Spring is the season of moving—the real estate market picks up, and "for sale" signs crop up in the neighborhood. Please bless all who are preparing for moves, that they find a house that can be a true home. Please bless those who are not moving by choice—those who are relocating for a spouse's job, or no longer able to maintain their home because of age. Please help us all remember that you go with us everywhere, and that we do not need to fear change when you are with us.

April 27

Blessed assurance, Jesus is mine!
Oh what a foretaste of glory divine!
Heir of salvation, purchase of God,
born of his Spirit, washed in his blood.
Perfect submission, perfect delight!
Visions of rapture now burst on my sight;
angels descending bring from above
echoes of mercy, whispers of love.
Perfect submission––all is at rest,
I in my Savior am happy and blest;
watching and waiting, looking above,
filled with his goodness, lost in his love.

This is my story, this is my song,
praising my Savior all the day long;
this is my story, this is my song,
praising my Savior all the day long.

—Fanny J. Crosby

April 28

In the mouth of the foolish is a rod of pride: but the lips of the wise shall preserve them.

—Proverbs 14:3

Lord, I knew the minute the words were out of my mouth that they would have been better left unsaid. Why do I continue to fall into the trap of needing to say what I think at the expense of someone else? Not only did I hurt someone's feelings, but I also looked like a fool in the process! Help me to repair the damage and learn from this experience. Give me another chance to behave nobly by saying nothing.

April 29

Have you ever been overwhelmed with gratitude toward God? Ever started singing a favorite hymn or worship song just because you wanted to let God know how much you love him? That's the work of God's spirit in us, filling us with praise, thanks, and love. These are precious offerings held in God's treasury of remembrance, just as we hold our own children's love gifts close to our hearts. Perhaps there is a love gift you would care to offer your heavenly Father even now as you consider his goodness.

April 30

I am grateful that you don't require spiritual gymnastics from me when I sin, Lord. You just call me to come to you with a humble and repentant heart. In my pride I sometimes want to do something that will impress you—something that will "make up for it" somehow. But you just shake your head and keep calling me to humble myself and bring my sincere sorrow to you. That often doesn't seem like enough to me. But I guess that's the point: I can never earn your grace; it is a gift. Christ died on the cross for us because it is beyond our powers to make up for all the sins we have committed. I bring my contrite heart before you now, Lord. Thank you for receiving it as an acceptable sacrifice.

May

May 1

And before I had done speaking in mine heart, behold, Rebekah came forth with her pitcher on her shoulder; and she went down unto the well, and drew water: and I said unto her, Let me drink, I pray thee.

—*Genesis 24:45-46*

A despairing heart mumbles, "God is doing nothing."
A hopeful heart inquires, "God, what are you going to do next?" and looks forward to celebrating God's awesome ingenuity.

May 2

Seeking courage, Lord, I bundle my fears and place them in your hands.
Too heavy for me, too weighty even to ponder in this moment,
such shadowy terrors shrink to size in my mind and—how
wonderful!—wither to nothing in your grasp.

May 3

Lord,
I like the part about "new" and "better,"
But what's that going to look like? Feel like?
What's all this going to mean?
I want transformation,
but the change part scares me.
Give me strength, Lord.
Help me accept your gift of new life.
Lead me forward.
I put my trust in you.
Amen.

May 4

If thou, Lord, shouldest mark iniquities, O Lord, who shall stand?
But there is forgiveness with thee, that thou mayest be feared.
I wait for the Lord, my soul doth wait, and in his word do I hope.
—Psalm 130:3–5

God's desire for love from us is not primarily for his benefit, but for ours. One of his deepest desires is that we know his love, and somehow when we take action to love him, it is then we discover just how much he loves us.

May 5

The Lord did not set his love upon you, nor choose you, because ye were more in number than any people; for ye were the fewest of all people:

But because the Lord loved you, and because he would keep the oath which he had sworn unto your fathers, hath the Lord brought you out with a mighty hand, and redeemed you out of the house of bondmen, from the hand of Pharaoh king of Egypt.

—Deuteronomy 7:7-8

We sometimes fear drawing close to God, who is the source of love. Yet, when we finally choose to draw near, what a wonderful discovery we make—we are loved completely.

May 6

And Jesus went forth, and saw a great multitude, and was moved with compassion toward them, and he healed their sick.

—Matthew 14:14

When we see our enemies from God's perspective, compassion follows, for he has seen the sorrows in their hearts that have caused them to behave in such a manner. He longs to reach out to these people and comfort them, and he sometimes uses our hands to do it.

May 7

Sometimes there is pain involved in looking back, but there is also so much joy and so many things that fill our hearts with gratitude. Renew our dedication to living a life that brings you glory for as long as we are on this earth. Remind us of the rich heritage that is ours through you, and keep us both humble and grateful.

May 8

Lord, you are the God who has set the foundations of the earth, who blessed Abraham with offspring "as numerous as the stars in heaven." You have blessed me, too, by giving me the treasure of my heart, my family. I pour out my thanks for these gifts, which are far a bove any riches the world can give. How can I praise you enough?

Heavenly Father, I never fail to come to you for help and comfort in the dark times of my life, yet I don't always remember you when my cup is overflowing. Forgive me if I seem ungrateful and take your generosity for granted. How can I forget all that you give me each day? You bring beauty, peace, and love to my existence. My heart overflows with thanksgiving.

May 9

I confess, Lord, that in my haste to come to you in prayer and to present my daily laundry list of requests, I forget the other side of prayer. I forget to listen for your answer. I know that if I am patient enough, your gentle message will come to me when I wait for it.

Forgive me my impatience, Father, when I ask for your help with my children, then fail to listen to your response. Thank you for teaching me that if I seek, I will find. Help me to seek and listen for your answers, written across the pages of my heart.

May 10

Lord, so often it isn't until after a crisis has passed that we can see all the ways that you were present in the midst of it. Forgive us for focusing on the negative and missing your positive contributions. Remind us to expect your involvement—to actively watch for it, even! We need to be alert to the working of your spirit in all things and give thanks at all times.

May 11

Now therefore fear ye not: I will nourish you, and your little ones. And he comforted them, and spake kindly unto them.

—Genesis 50:21

When I'm waiting through the turmoil of doing the right thing at the cost of my personal comfort, Lord, help me to be patient. Help me not to sabotage your works by trying to fix things in my own way. Oh, it's not always easy to hold my tongue, but if I wait until you open the door for me to speak—and I look to you for the right attitude when I do talk—then I won't have to deal with all the regrets and what-ifs. Grant me a patient spirit, Father.

May 12

Thy mercy, O Lord, is in the heavens; and thy faithfulness reacheth unto the clouds.

—Psalm 36:5

Lord, please keep me from falling into the trap of placing any other human on a pedestal. Even the most spiritual-seeming religious leaders are riddled with imperfection; they struggle with sin, just as I do. You alone are perfect and pure, and you alone are worthy of my adoration. I promise I will not follow anyone else, no matter how spiritually enlightened they may seem. There is no one like you, and you are the only one who will ever have my full devotion.

May 13

And David danced before the Lord with all his might; and David was girded with a linen ephod.

—2 Samuel 6:14

All around leaves are falling, drifting, swooping in the wind. They become a whirligig, a dance of wind and nature. They are a picture of the heavenly places where lighthearted beings are carried by the invisible power of love.

May 14

Sometimes in the hazy morning between "waking up" and "not yet," take the time to listen to your own soul. You'll find you can hear your angels telling you to be ready for the day. It's the best wake-up call there is.

May 15

Lord you are tiptoeing on tiny infant feet to find us. May we drop whatever we're doing and accept this gesture of a baby so small it may get overlooked in our frantic search for something massive and overwhelming. Remind us that it is not you who demands lavish celebrations. Rather, you ask only that we have the faith of a mustard seed and willingness to let a small hand take ours. We are ready.

May 16

Although our eyes should always be turned above toward God, sometimes we can do with a reminder of God's work just a little bit closer to home. The faith of others can serve as a reminder or an inspiration to strengthen our own faith. Just as we should provide encouragement to others, we can draw on others to help steady ourselves.

May 17

And God saw the light, that it was good: and God divided the light from the darkness.

—Genesis 1:4

I am feeling my way in this darkness, God, and it seems I'm going in circles. Yet you have reminded me—quietly, just now—that encircled by your love with every move in any direction I go no closer to you—nor farther either—than already centered I am.

May 18

Most of us realize that we are naturally self-centered, and we often respond to those around us in ways that make us appear proud, haughty, or arrogant. But if we look at Jesus' life, we see an excellent example of humility—an example that we should strive to follow. He taught that pride was destructive, but humility was powerful. Rather than touting his own greatness, Jesus was willing to kneel down and wash the feet of others, to show that we should all be servants to each other—and to God.

May 19

And he charged them, saying, Thus shall ye do in the fear of the Lord, faithfully, and with a perfect heart.

—2 Chronicles 19:9

If our faith was never tested, how would we know we had any? When things go wrong and we can still say, "I believe in God no matter what happens," we show our faith to be real.

May 20

Sometimes I'm like Peter,
and I walk on water.
I stand above my circumstances,
which are like the swirling tempests of the sea.
But then, like Peter,
I take my eyes off Jesus
and concentrate on things below.
Soon I start to sink.
How I long to have
a consistent
water-walking
eyes-on-Jesus
faith.

May 21

Shall thy lovingkindness be declared in the grave? or thy faithfulness in destruction?

—*Psalm 88:15*

When a task requiring faith confronts us, voices around us may say, "It can't be done." The voice may even come from within us, and we may want to quit before we start. But if we hold on to faith, we can succeed, no matter what the critics say.

May 22

If my people, which are called by my name, shall humble themselves,
and pray, and seek my face, and turn from their wicked ways; then will
I hear from heaven, and will forgive their sin, and will heal their land.

—2 Chronicles 7:14

Sometimes the best way to humble ourselves is just to walk outside and see everything God has created. A daily walk provides a peaceful way to focus on the world outside ourselves.

May 23

Lord, you come to us in the storm, the fire, and even in the stillness of a quiet moment. Sometimes your message is strong, carried on bustling angelic wings; sometimes our spirits are nudged, our hearts lightened by the gentle whisper of spirit voices. However, you approach us, your message is always one of tender love and compassion. Thank you for the certainty—and the surprise—of your holy voice.

May 24

Be of good courage, and he shall strengthen your heart, all ye that hope in the Lord.

—*Psalm 31:24*

Help me to see with new eyes today—especially the burden of care that others harbor within them. Grant me insight to see beyond smiling faces into hearts that hurt. And when I recognize the pain, Lord, let me reach out.

May 25

What is my strength, that I should hope? and what is mine end, that I should prolong my life?

—Job 6:11

I wish to be of service, Lord. So, give me courage to put my own hope and despair, my own doubt and fear at the disposal of others. For how could I ever help without first being simply...real?

May 26

Bless our differences, O Lord. And let us love across all barriers, the walls we build of color, culture, and language. Let us turn our eyes upward and remember: The God who made us all lives and breathes and moves within us, untouched by our petty distinctions. Let us love him as he is, for he loves us just as we are.

May 27

Waiting,
endless waiting.
Why does it seem impossible
to wait patiently
and
graciously—
   for the overdue phone call
   or the long-expected letter...
   for delayed company to arrive
   or a sick loved one to get better?
Is there a special ingredient
to fill the waiting time
and ease the heavy burdens
that weigh upon my mind?

Could waiting possibly achieve a work
which nothing else can do?
God, teach me how to
wait patiently
and put full trust
in you.

May 28

An honest man is not a man who never lies. There is no such man. When an honest man is caught in a lie or discovers he has lied, he is quick to admit it. He then speaks the truth. He's not afraid to say, "Please forgive me for not being honest." He does not defend a lie. Unlike a dishonest man, he does not make plans to lie or use lies to cover other falsehoods. He regularly scrutinizes his life to see if he has lied or is living a lie in any area. Honesty with God, his fellow man, and himself is the honest man's goal and his heart's desire.

May 29

Rejoice when I run into problems?
Know trials are good for me?
Things like that aren't easy—
learning to live patiently.

Growing in grace is a process.
Developing character hurts.
Becoming more Christ-like in all things
is an everyday process called work.

But if I have faith it is possible.
Faith knowing God loves and cares—
that all my burdens and trials
he also feels and shares.

May 30

Now Israel loved Joseph more than all his children, because he was the son of his old age: and he made him a coat of many colors.

—*Genesis 37:3*

To find love, we think we must first find the courage to take a big chance by risking our heart to another; yet it's only then that we discover it's in the very act of offering ourselves that love is found.

May 31

But that on the good ground are they, which in an honest and good heart, having heard the word, keep it, and bring forth fruit with patience.

—Luke 8:15

We can never be completely honest on our own. It is human nature to lie. That's why when a witness who takes the stand in a court of law is asked, "Do you solemnly swear to tell the truth, the whole truth, and nothing but the truth," the phrase is added, "so help me God."

June

June 1

And be ye kind one to another, tenderhearted, forgiving one another, even as God for Christ's sake hath forgiven you.

—*Ephesians 4:32*

To love means always to act with kindness and in the best interests of the other person. We may have to do things that will hurt one another, but only out of necessity, and only with the greatest honesty and compassion.

June 2

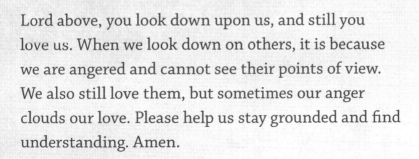

Lord above, you look down upon us, and still you love us. When we look down on others, it is because we are angered and cannot see their points of view. We also still love them, but sometimes our anger clouds our love. Please help us stay grounded and find understanding. Amen.

June 3

Lead me, O Lord, in thy righteousness because of mine enemies; make thy way straight before my face. For there is no faithfulness in their mouth; their inward part is very wickedness; their throat is an open sepulchre; they flatter with their tongue.

—*Psalm 5:8-9*

Faith in a wise and trustworthy God, even in broken times like these, teaches us a new math: subtracting old ways and adding new thoughts because sharing with God divides our troubles and multiplies unfathomable possibilities for renewed life.

June 4

I am like two halves of a walnut, God. I am of two minds: despairing and hopeful. Help me to feel your hand holding me together as I rebuild my life when at first it seemed too hard to even try. In order to get to the meat of a walnut, it must be split into halves. May the brokenness I feel get me to the nourishment—the meat—I need in order to move on. Amen.

June 5

For the Son of man is come to save that which was lost.

—Matthew 18:11

Confusion is directing my thoughts. My mind loyally follows its erratic demands and becomes increasingly lost and frustrated. I need a sign to orient myself and to find my way out of this turmoil. Find me, Lord, for I am wandering in the wilderness of my own mind, heading deeper and deeper into despair. *Where are you?* I call. And then I realize that by describing my lostness, you show me where I am and how to return home.

June 6

And a third part shall be at the gate of Sur; and a third part at the gate behind the guard: so shall ye keep the watch of the house, that it be not broken down.

— *2 Kings 11:6*

We are grateful, O God, for glimpses we are given of you during times like these. Thank you for showing us how, during raging winds, the mother cardinal refuses to move, standing like a mighty shelter over the fledglings beneath her wings. Secure us in the truth that we, the children of your heart, are likewise watched over and protected during life's storms.

June 7

Life becomes much easier and more enjoyable when we know we are never alone. We always have our Higher Power to turn to for strength, hope, guidance, and renewal. God is on the job 24 hours a day, 7 days a week, 365 days a year.

June 8

Lord, you do not leave us to suffer alone. You are with us in pain, in sickness, and in our worst moments. Thank you for your comfort and healing power. Thank you for getting us through when our bodies fail, when our health falters, and when we need you most of all. Amen.

June 9

And if thou say in thine heart, Wherefore come these things upon me?
For the greatness of thine iniquity are thy skirts discovered
 and thy heels made bare.

—Jeremiah 13:22

Inspired by you, Great God, and grateful for the unique gifts
we're discovering, we toss ourselves into the stream of life to
make ripples wherever we are. In your hands, our gifts can offer a
gift that keeps on making ever-widening circles to reach all those
stranded on shore.

June 10

And he said, What meanest thou by all this drove which I met? And he said, These are to find grace in the sight of my lord.

—Genesis 33:8

Each of us can turn within to connect with an amazing place full of amazing grace. This is where God lives. This is where we live. This is our soul.

Each of us can turn within to connect with an amazing grace where God lives.

June 11

And the Lord God called unto Adam, and said unto him,
Where art thou?

—Genesis 3:9

The answer to senseless destruction is purposeful creation.

Art, in all its forms, is a great healer.

If you can write, write.

If you can paint, paint.

If you're a potter, turn pots.

You are a child of God, so fill your life with creation.

June 12

And he will love thee, and bless thee, and multiply thee: he will also bless the fruit of thy womb, and the fruit of thy land, thy corn, and thy wine, and thine oil, the increase of thy kine, and the flocks of thy sheep, in the land which he sware unto thy fathers to give thee.

—Deuteronomy 7:13

Love is an active force. When we "walk our talk" and live God's message of love, we create a person full of faith. When we do that, we are God's voice, his hands, his light for each other. We are living love.

June 13

Like the turkey wishbone, God of wholeness, I am being pulled apart by job, family, home, errands, friends, and my needs. I'm preoccupied with what I am not doing and feel the pull to do it all. Help me choose wisely. Remind me to negotiate on the job and at home for the time I need in both places. Remind me, O God, to negotiate for a leaner lifestyle, for I am part of the pull. In the tugging days ahead, be the hinge that keeps my life's parts synchronized in harmonious movement, not split apart at all.

June 14

Security, loving God, is going to sleep in the assurance that you know our hearts before we speak and are waiting, as soon as you hear from us, to transform our concerns into hope and action, our loneliness into companionship, and our despair into dance.

June 15

And I will bless her, and give thee a son also of her: yea, I will bless her, and she shall be a mother of nations; kings of people shall be of her.

—*Genesis 17:16*

Stand in a beloved's shade, not shadow, and discover new sights to share, new directions to go, all leading to even more reasons for standing together.

June 16

Held up to your light, our broken hearts can become prisms that scatter micro-rainbows on the wall. Our pain is useless as it is, redeeming God, just as a prism is a useless chunk of glass until light passes through it. Remind us that the smallest ray of sun in a shower can create a rainbow. Use our tears as the showers and your love as the sun. Looking up, we see the tiniest arches of hope in the lightening sky.

June 17

*And thou shalt have joy and gladness; and many shall
rejoice at his birth.*

—Luke 1:14

Dear God, complaints sometimes come first before I can feel free
to love you. Sometimes you seem distant and unreasonable, un-
caring. Help me understand why life can be so hurtful and hard.
Hear my complaints and, in the spirit of compassion, show me
how to move through pain to rebirth.

June 18

And the whole multitude sought to touch him: for there went virtue out of him, and healed them all.

—Luke 6:19

A chart of my efforts to change traces a jagged course, Lord, like the lines on a heart-rate monitor. Reassure me that instead of measuring my failures, ups and downs mean simply that I am alive and ever-changing. Help me become consistent, but deliver me from flat lines.

June 19

For I have said, Mercy shall be built up for ever: thy faithfulness shalt thou establish in the very heavens.

—Psalm 89:2

You have made things problematic again, Lord, and I need to see that all this upheaval can be a good thing. Help me, Lord. And thank you for showing me that a thoroughly comfortable existence can rob me of real life.

June 20

You are everywhere, Lord, and we're comforted to be enfolded as we move through life's extremes. You are with us in birthings and dyings, in routine and surprise, and in stillness and activity. We cannot wander so far in any direction that you are not already there.

June 21

In this world where human love is conditional and often temporary, it is a joy to know that God loves us unconditionally and eternally. Nothing we can say or do will cause him to stop loving us. Our minds cannot even imagine the immensity of his love for each person on this planet. He sent his son to earth to deliver that message of love personally. When he died for us, he was saying through his action, "I love you." God remains always ready to lavish his love on his children. May you open your heart to receive all the love he has to offer.

June 22

And the priest shall make an atonement for him before the Lord: and it shall be forgiven him for any thing of all that he hath done in trespassing therein.

—Leviticus 6:7

My guard is constant and vigilant, protecting me against the next episode of my humanness. I know to error is human, but why so often? Peace only comes, God of wholeness, through reassurance that with you, mistakes, errors—even disasters—can yield treasures. I am so grateful.

June 23

Whereby are given unto us exceeding great and precious promises: that by these ye might be partakers of the divine nature, having escaped the corruption that is in the world through lust.

—2 Peter 1:4

Help me take stock of your gifts to me, Lord. I'm good at things that appear to be so insignificant. Chances are you can use any one of them, no matter how simple it appears, to help others. Remind me that it's not what I do but my doing that ultimately matters.

June 24

He maketh the storm a calm, so that the waves thereof are still.

—Psalm 107:29

If happiness consists in the number of pleasing emotions that occupy our mind—how true is it that the contemplation of nature, which always gives rise to these emotions, is one of the great sources of happiness.

Thomas Belt

June 25

There is in your grace, God of second chances, insufficient evidence to prove my latest setback is a failure. Even if it is, with you, failure is never final but an opportunity to learn and grow. When I goof, as I am prone to do, help me from doubling the problem by failing to take advantage of your redemption.

June 26

The past, O God of yesterdays, todays, and promise-filled tomorrows, can be an anchor or a launching pad. It's sometimes so easy to look back on the pain and hurt and believe the future may be an instant replay. Help us to accept the aches of the past and put them in perspective so we can also see the many ways you supported and nurtured us. Then, believing in your promise of regeneration, launch us into the future free and excited to live in joy.

June 27

Left alone now, we drift aimlessly like untied balloons let loose to fly helter-skelter. Yet life goes on, decisions must be made. O God, help us make up minds that won't stay still. Give us good sense to put off until tomorrow what we shouldn't try today. Reassure us this is only temporary, a brief hesitation, not a giving up; hold up a mirror for us to see a once-again clear-eyed person.

June 28

Just when I settle in with one reality, something new disrupts. Overnight change, God of all the time in the world, is comforting and grief-making, for it's a reminder that nothing stays the same. Not tough times, not good ones either. Despite today's annoyance, I'm grateful for change, assured it will take me to new moments you have in mind.

June 29

But even the very hairs of your head are all numbered. Fear not therefore: ye are of more value than many sparrows.

— Luke 12:7

Sticks and stones of prejudice feel like they're breaking bones. Yet God calls us by name, numbers the hairs on our heads, guards our comings in and goings out, lifts us to high places and sets angels over us. How can we doubt our value with such overwhelming evidence to the contrary!

June 30

Who was my sorrow for
last week when from my mud-room door
I watched an arrogant mallard drake,
from a wintering-over flock of eight,
fly to my lawn from a nearby lake.
He stumbled, injured,
right leg strong, left folding down.
I watched that green-headed, curly-tailed drake
hesitate. Then, heeding a hen's loud call,
he hobbled to corn scattered near a garden wall.
Oh, God, I am injured, too
my sorrows slow to mend.
But today, as I turned from the mud-room door
came the call of a faithful friend.

July

July 1

We're tempted to give up until we see the geese. God provided them a "V" in which to fly, a main "point" goose providing wind resistance for followers. Geese take turns, take up slack, in the natural rhythm of things. When we ask for help, we let someone else take the point position. And we feel an updraft of air to rest in, and feel God in this current of wind.

July 2

Be strong and of a good courage, fear not, nor be afraid of them: for the Lord thy God, he it is that doth go with thee; he will not fail thee, nor forsake thee.

— *Deuteronomy 3:16*

Help me understand, Lord, that the courage I am praying for is not dry-eyed stoicism and perky denial. Courage is not hiding my feelings, even from you, and putting on a brave false face. Rather it is facing facts, weighing options, and moving ahead. No need to waste precious time pretending.

July 3

To the Lord our God belong mercies and forgivenesses, though we
have rebelled against him; Neither have we obeyed the voice of
the Lord our God, to walk in his laws, which he set before us by his
servants the prophets.

— *Daniel 9:9–10*

When things go wrong, God is usually the first we blame. Forgive us for even considering that you would deliberately hurt one of your very own children. For what could you possibly have to gain? Thank you for your presence; forgive our easy blame of you.

July 4

How blessed I am to live in the United States! Life may not always be easy, but I am grateful for the freedoms this nation gives to me. Thank you, Lord, for all the people who fought to make this country a free and beautiful land. I remember those patriots today as I listen to fireworks and enjoy my freedom. May I never take that freedom for granted.

July 5

Life's not fair, and I stomp my foot in frustration. The powerful get more so as the rest of us shrink, dreams for peace are shattered as bullies get the upper hand, and despair is as tempting as an ice cream sundae. Help me hold on, for you are a God of justice and dreams, of turning life upside down. Let me help; thanks for listening in the meantime.

July 6

What, God of peace, are we to do with our anger? In the wake of trouble, it fills us to overflowing. Sometimes our anger is the only prayer we can bring you. We are relieved and grateful to know that you are sturdy enough to bear all we feel and say. Where do we go from here? Is there life after fury? What will we be without our anger when it's all that has fueled us? When we are still, we hear your answer: "Emptied." But then we would be nothing. Remind us that, in your redeeming hands, nothing can become of great use, as a gourd hollowed out becomes a cup or a bowl only when emptied. When the time comes for us to empty ourselves of this abundance of anger, make us into something useful. It would be a double tragedy to waste anger's re-creative energy.

July 7

For he commandeth, and raiseth the stormy wind, which lifteth up the
waves thereof.

— Psalm 107:25

May you be assured of God's presence as you weather this storm.
As the waves toss you about, and the ship of your life threatens
to crash into rough rocks: He is there. Never despair. For no wind
or water, rock or sand has the power to defeat his plans for you.
And, after all, he created all these things, and in him alone they
have their existence.

July 8

O Lord, hear my prayer for all who are in trouble this day. Comfort those who are facing the loss of a loved one. After the wrenching grief, let their lonely hours be filled with fond memories of days gone by. Let your hope fill their hearts as they recall all your past faithfulness. Heal those who are suffering pain and illness. Let them find rest and calm as they seek to make the idle moments pass more quickly; racked in mind and stressed-out emotionally. Cradle their minds in your love and soothe every irrational thought that seeks to run out of control. Uphold those who are being tempted in any way today. Especially those who may want to end their lives. Show them that while there is life there is hope, that change is the only constant, and that change for the better is so likely. May they find joy in just one moment at a time. And may that be enough for now. In all these ways I ask your blessing upon those in trouble. And please include me in that blessing, too!

July 9

Then Isaac sowed in that land, and received in the same year an hundredfold: and the Lord blessed him.

— *Genesis 26:12*

May you find joy and satisfaction in your family life: in building a home and setting up a residence—be blessed! in finding a job and working diligently—be blessed! in taking care of little ones and making friends in the neighborhood—be blessed! in seeking God for all your help and guidance, bringing every care to him, yes, I pray, may you indeed be blessed.

July 10

My God, I thank you for the blessings of the single life.
One of your plans was for people to get married and have
children. But I know that your good and perfect will is also
for some of us to live unmarried and not have children.

For this life I thank you. For the gift to be free to learn to
love without clinging. To seek relationships without owning,
to offer my love and kindness among many friends.

Yes, Lord at times I am lonely, like all people can be.
So I ask you to fill those times of emptiness with your
presence. Enter into the barren places with your refreshing
water of life.

And as I continue on this path—living by myself—keep
my friends and family close, no matter how far away they
live. Give me peace in my daily work, joy in the pursuit of
wholeness, and comfort in the solitary nights. And please
continue to give me a giving heart.

For I know, Lord, I am blessed.

July 11

And when the woman of Tekoah spake to the king, she fell on her face to the ground, and did obeisance, and said, Help, O king.

— 2 Samuel 14:4

O God, you have called each of us to special tasks, purposes, and vocations, equipping us with the skills and energy to perform them. For some, our vocations send us into the labor force; for some, it is soon bringing retirement. For some, it is in full-time homemaking. For some, our vocations are in artistic skills; for some, in volunteering, helping, neighboring. Always, there is that first call from you, God of vision, working through our work to help, heal, change a needful world.

July 12

The blessing of him that was ready to perish came upon me: and I caused the widow's heart to sing for joy.

— Job 29:13

How boring these meaningless details! Is this really what work is meant to be? Can you make it sing again? Put the spark back in my zeal? Because I know that work is a blessed privilege; I don't want to be ungrateful. But how boring the piles of paperwork, how deadening the countless reports, how fatiguing the endless round of meetings. Yes, I need to feel it again, Lord—the joy. Help!

July 13

Be of good courage, and let us play the men for our people, and for the cities of our God: and the Lord do that which seemeth him good.

— *2 Samuel 10:12*

Achievers, it is said, spend nights on the office couch snuggled up with work. Should we all follow suit?

Lord, lead us past the temptation to sleep on the job, literally and figuratively. Grant us the good sense to know when to lock up and go home. There's nothing like a good night's sleep in our own beds, surrounded by snoring family, to get us ready for work tomorrow, refreshed and eager for your call to excellence. Goodnight, Lord, time to call it a day.

July 14

My heart is fixed, O God, my heart is fixed: I will sing and give praise.

— *Psalm 57:7*

When life goes awry, Lord, I need someone to blame so I
point the finger at you. Heaven help me, I want it both ways:
you as sender and fixer of trouble. Help me know you don't will
trouble, for what could you possibly gain? And when the good
you want for me isn't possible in the randomness of life, I know
you are with me.

July 15

Behold, we count them happy which endure. Ye have heard of the patience of Job, and have seen the end of the Lord; that the Lord is very pitiful, and of tender mercy.

— James 5:11

May you come to know that God is your friend. When you feel a frowning face is looking down at you from heaven, recall that nothing you could do could ever make God love you more or love you less. He simply loves—completely, perfectly. So feel the blessedness of that!

July 16

*You created your world as a circle of love, designer God,
a wonderful round globe of beauty. And you create
us still today in circles of love—families, friendships,
communities. Yet your circle of love is repeatedly broken
because of our love of exclusion. We make separate circles:
inner circle and outer circle; circle of power and circle
of despair; circle of privilege and circle of deprivation.
We need your healing touch to smooth our sharp edges.
Remind us that only a fully round, hand-joined circle
can move freely like a spinning wheel or
the globe we call home.*

July 17

We come, needing your help to move beyond: the times we hurt one another and the times we willingly misunderstand, cherishing our differences and the times we assume we know all there is to know about each other and turn away. And then there are the times that we make private rules only to publicly condemn anyone who fails to abide by them, limiting one another by labeling, interpreting, conditioning, insisting, resisting, defining. From all this, Lord, we come, asking that you forgive us as we forgive those "others" we need new eyes to see and ears to hear. Be with us as we do so.

July 18

And there shalt thou build an altar unto the Lord thy God, an altar of stones: thou shalt not lift up any iron tool upon them.

— Deuteronomy 27:5

Bless me with the kind heart of a peacemaker and a builder's sturdy hand, Lord, for these are mean-spirited, litigious times when we tear down with words and weapons first and ask questions later. Help me take every opportunity to compliment, praise, and applaud as I rebuild peace.

July 19

And in thy seed shall all the nations of the earth be blessed; because thou hast obeyed my voice.

— Genesis 22:18

Bless those who mentor, model, and cheer me on, Lord, urging me toward goals I set, applauding as I reach them, and nourishing me to try again when I don't. Remind me to be a cheerleader. I plan to say thanks to those who are mine.

July 20

*For there is hope of a tree, if it be cut down, that it will sprout again,
and that the tender branch thereof will not cease.*

— Job 14:7

Hope is the aspiration of the soul,
the persistence of the mind,
and the affirmation of the heart.

July 21

Lord of my heart, give me a refreshing drink from the fountains of your love, walking through this desert as I have. Lord of my heart, spread out before me a new vision of your goodness, locked into this dull routine as I was. Lord of my heart, lift up a shining awareness of your will and purpose, awash in doubts and fears though I be.

July 22

Spirit of God, keep teaching me the ways of change and growth. Like the wind, you cannot be tracked or traced. The breezes blow where they will: silently, invisibly, with great power. Just as you are working in lives even now. Let me know your calling as you move in me! Yes, whisk with your persistent prompting through all the windows of my soul, the dark corners of my heart.

July 23

And they shall keep his charge, and the charge of the whole congregation before the tabernacle of the congregation, to do the service of the tabernacle.

— Numbers 3:7

Keep us connected, O God of all time, to those who've come before. Inspire us to tell family tales and to pull out family albums and family Bibles and handed-down antiques to show the connecting links of which your love forges us into a whole.

July 24

In all things, give thanks. In the good days of laughter and joy, give thanks.

In the bad days of struggle and strife, give thanks.

In the brightest moments and the darkest hours, give thanks.

In the flow of blessings and the apparent lack of goodness, give thanks.

In the face of fortune and misfortune, give thanks.

In the presence of pleasure and pain, give thanks.

In all things, give thanks.

For lessons and blessings are found not just in the light, but in the darkness.

July 25

And he dreamed yet another dream, and told it his brethren, and said,
Behold, I have dreamed a dream more; and, behold, the sun and the
moon and the eleven stars made obeisance to me.

— Genesis 37:9

I always want to be a dreamer, O God, to feel the stir and
the yearning to see my vision become reality. There are those
who would say dreamers are free-floaters. When I dream I feel
connected to you and to your creation, bound by purpose
and a sense of call. Nourish my dreams and my striving to
make them real.

July 26

And he took the book of the covenant, and read in the audience of the people: and they said, All that the Lord hath said will we do, and be obedient.

— Exodus 24:7

Your son, Jesus, was a reader, Lord. He read from your own books, the Holy Scriptures. Books can change us. They can transport us to other places and other times and can share the wisdom of the ages. I love books and reading and want my children to treasure them, too. Thank you, Lord, for good books, especially the Bible, that can feed our children's minds and imaginations and can show us the wonder of life in your world.

July 27

Wait on the Lord: be of good courage, and he shall strengthen thine heart: wait, I say, on the Lord.

— *Psalm 27:14*

Sometimes my doubts are so strong and so bothersome. Give me courage to express my doubts to you, O God, knowing that they are necessary moments through which I can pass on my way to true contentment in you.

July 28

In this day of bigger is best, Lord, we wonder what difference our little lights can make. Remind us of the laser, so tiny, yet when focused, has infinite power. This little light of mine, O Lord, give it such focus.

July 29

And God made the firmament, and divided the waters which were under the firmament from the waters which were above the firmament: and it was so.

— *Genesis 1:7*

Touch and calm my turbulent emotions, God of the still waters. Whisper words to the listening ears of my soul. In hearing your voice, give me assurance beyond a shadow of a doubt that you are my companion in life, eternally.

July 30

*My sister's courage doesn't conquer empires. It is the courage to go on despite lost empires and lost love and lost hope. It is the courage to get up every morning, look the day straight in the eye, and say,
"I will live with all my heart."*

July 31

Arise; for this matter belongeth unto thee: we also will be with thee: be of good courage, and do it.

— *Ezra 10:4*

I get discouraged, O God, my comforter and guide, and feel overwhelmed, which makes me even more discouraged. Lead me beyond negative thoughts and useless circles of worry to a renewed frame of mind. Work your miracle of transformation in me.

August

August 1

Lord, I've learned how to pray in strange but necessary places: in car pools, while cooking dinner, at the dentist, between loads of laundry, waiting in the checkout line. I've discovered that it's not how long I pray that matters but rather the very act of attempting to make a connection with you.

August 2

And Isaac brought her into his mother Sarah's tent, and took Rebekah, and she became his wife; and he loved her: and Isaac was comforted after his mother's death.

— *Genesis 24:67*

A mother, a rosebud, early in the morning, dew still on her petals, begins her work, unfurling as the sun shines higher, with more beauty every minute, making the thorns of life lovely, freshening the summer air, making this world a beautiful place.

August 3

And Pharaoh said unto his servants, Can we find such a one as this is,
a man in whom the Spirit of God is?

— *Genesis 41:38*

Lord, help me remember that you are the God of hope. You don't
want me to feel sad or hopeless. It isn't your plan for me to live
in fear or doubt. Help me to feel and access the power of the Holy
Spirit. I know that through your spirit I will find the hope and joy
and peace you have promised to your people.

August 4

Lord, it is sometimes hard to love those around me when they are so different in their beliefs and behaviors. I find myself sometimes feeling intolerant, even afraid. But you gave me the commandment to love others as myself, and that if I love you, then I love all of your creation. Help me to open my heart and my mind to those I see as being different, and find in them the common light of your presence. Help me to be a better person and not fear others just because they are not like me. Help me to see the wonder and magic in learning about others and letting them learn about me.

August 5

And God blessed them, saying, Be fruitful, and multiply, and fill the
waters in the seas, and let fowl multiply in the earth.

— Genesis 1:22

Because God is good, he loves to bless us, but his deepest longing
is for a relationship with us.

As you enjoy the good things the heavenly Father has given to
you, take time to commune with him, to grow closer to him, and
to get to know him a little better.

August 6

And shewing mercy unto thousands of them that love me and keep my commandments.

— *Deuteronomy 5:10*

Lord, you are the foundation of my life. When circumstances shift and make my world unsteady, you remain firm. When threats of what lies ahead blow against the framework of my thoughts, you are solid. When I focus on your steadfastness, I realize that you are my strength for the moment, the one sure thing in my life. Because of you I stand now, and I will stand tomorrow as well, because you are there already. Amen.

August 7

And it shall come to pass, if they will not believe thee, neither
hearken to the voice of the first sign, that they will believe
the voice of the latter sign.

— Exodus 4:8

God of my life, though you are not visible to me, I see evidence of your existence everywhere I look. You speak to me in silent ways with an inaudible voice. How can I explain this mystery—what I know to be true but cannot prove? This spiritual sensitivity—this awareness of you—is more real to me than the pages on which my eyes fall at this moment. You exist, and I believe.

August 8

Thou hast also given me the shield of thy salvation: and thy gentleness hath made me great.

— 2 Samuel 22:36

Heavenly Father, your son, Jesus, could have called down heaven to destroy his enemies when he was on earth, but he didn't. Revenge wasn't his mission. Love was. Help me to submit, as he did, to a path of gentleness in the strength of your love. Amen.

August 9

I feel free in your love, God. I feel as if I can live free from others' opinions, free from guilt, and free from fear because no matter what, your love is there for me. But I know that freedom can be abused, so help me remember that I also have been freed from the tyranny of fear, hatred, and arrogance. Help me exercise self-discipline so that I do not enslave myself to foolish extremes you never intended for me. Show me how to remain free and to lead others into your sanctuary of peace and freedom. Amen.

August 10

Those people who are unlikable to me, Lord, are not worthless, though I'm tempted to believe my self-centered thoughts about them. Rather, Lord, these people are precious works of beauty, created by you. And if I bother to look beyond my first impressions, I will be delighted by what I see of you in them.

August 11

But the fruit of the Spirit is love, joy, peace, longsuffering, gentleness,
goodness, faith, Meekness, temperance: against such there is no law.

— Galatians 5:22-23

O God, your love is so great. I'm not sure that I can love as you do
or even love others in a way that will please you. God, teach me
how to really love my family, my friends, and even strangers. I
trust in the power of your love to make me into a far more loving
person than I am today. Amen.

August 12

For where your treasure is, there will your heart be also.

— *Matthew 6:21*

Dear heavenly Father, I truly want to do good toward others. I don't want to just talk about being good, but I desire to be more compassionate. God, I need for you to teach me to be far more sensitive to the needs and sorrows of the people you have placed in my life and to be kind and encouraging toward them. I need for you to teach me how to truly love. I pray for this with all my heart. Amen.

August 13

And Moses said, Thou must give us also sacrifices and burnt offerings,
that we may sacrifice unto the Lord our God.

— Exodus 10:25

God, you gave up your own beloved son for me. How could I
possibly love with such a sense of sacrifice? Help me be the
kind of person who can put the needs of others before my own.
Help me give until it hurts. You have sacrificed for me—now
let me give of myself in return. I know that in the end, I will be
rewarded with your merciful grace. Amen.

August 14

Today, heavenly Father, you may call upon me to listen to someone and hear that person's heart. It may be someone who needs to feel significant enough to be heard, or perhaps someone who is lonely and longs to be connected to another person, or maybe someone who is hurting and needs a sympathetic ear. Whatever the case, Lord, please open my ears so I may listen to someone today. Amen.

August 15

Lord, I open my eyes and all I see are the amazing blessings that surround me. In this moment, I want for nothing, and I live with the knowledge that I can always turn to you for help, and cast my cares upon you, when my clarity and my vision cloud with worry. Thank you, Lord, for reminding me that the joyful blessings of this moment are all because of your love for me.

August 16

And Jacob called the name of the place Peniel: for I have seen God face to face, and my life is preserved.

— *Genesis 32:30*

When life seems dark and empty
and there's no hope in sight,
look for God to send an angel
to guide you toward the light.

August 17

And Shechem said unto her father and unto her brethren, Let me find grace in your eyes, and what ye shall say unto me I will give.

— Genesis 34:11

How often do we make plans, only to have them fall apart? When my day doesn't turn out the way I planned, it's easy to become angry. Instead, I look for ways to make the day special in a different way and thank God for showing me a new path. Lord, teach me to have a flexible heart and be willing to spend my time as you see fit, not as I do, and to open my eyes to the beauty of the unexpected.

August 18

Who guides and protects me in my life? Today, I am grateful for the people who have brought me to where I am today and who always have my best interests at heart. I may not always have appreciated their guidance, but I know deep down they always meant well. In the same way, Lord, let me accept and appreciate your guidance in my life.

August 19

Howbeit when he, the Spirit of truth, is come, he will guide you into all truth: for he shall not speak of himself; but whatsoever he shall hear, that shall he speak: and he will shew you things to come.

— John 16:13

I look around and see there is work to be done. Thank you for the gift of work to do. Guide my hands that they may help others. Guide my heart to see where there is need and how to respond to it. Guide my thoughts to know that even if I can only do a little, that is enough to make a difference.

August 20

*Thou shalt therefore keep this ordinance in his season
from year to year.*

— *Exodus 13:10*

Thank you for the bright colors of summer! I look around and see
the sun in the sky, the clear moon in the night, the brilliance of
the flowers and the trees. Thank you, Lord, for blessing me with
color in my life. I know that even the darkest, dreariest days
cannot last forever, just as the memory of winter fades during
summer's glory.

August 21

And Esau said unto his father, Hast thou but one blessing, my father? bless me, even me also, O my father. And Esau lifted up his voice, and wept.

— Genesis 27:38

The noise of my children fills my heart. I rejoice in their laughter and loud voices. Some days I may not appreciate the tumult children bring into my life. Help me to appreciate their moods, even when they are not always bright and happy. Lead me to be grateful for how much fun childhood can be. Thank you for letting me join my children in enjoying this special time.

August 22

In him was life; and the life was the light of men.

— *John 1:4*

Today I feel alone, yet I am not lonely. There is peace in solitude and rejuvenation in the quiet of being alone. Lead my thoughts to restful healing, Lord. Help me use this time alone to find myself and reach deep inside my heart and mind to find peace. I rejoice in being away from the noise and clatter of everyday life and praise God for letting me have this time for myself.

August 23

And with them Heman and Jeduthun with trumpets and cymbals for
those that should make a sound, and with musical instruments of God.

— 1 Chronicles 15:16

Music fills my heart today! I am so grateful for music in all its
forms: the loud thump of rock music, the pretty complexities of a
classical symphony, the simple melody of a whistled tune. Thank
you, God, for putting music into the world and letting it fill my
heart with emotion.

August 24

Today I take joy in nature. I look around and see all that you have made. The natural world is full of your presence. Thank you for the birds migrating overhead, for the wind's breath, even for the violence of a thunderstorm. I know that everything came to be by your hand, and the world around me is a blessing in my life.

August 25

Rain patters down, making puddles everywhere. I wasn't expecting the rain, but I am grateful for its beauty. I look up and see the thickness of the gray clouds and think of a soft blanket. I listen to the rain pour down and think of how it waters the earth to bring new life. Thank you, Lord, for the gift of a rainy day.

August 26

Thank you for my community. As I run my errands and conduct my business, let me remember to be grateful for everyone who helps me. From a clerk at the store to the police officer keeping me safe, my community is filled with people who help others. Thank you, Lord, for putting these people in my life and for giving me the chance to know them. May I always work to make my community a better place.

August 27

And they said, Go to, let us build us a city and a tower, whose top may reach unto heaven; and let us make us a name, lest we be scattered abroad upon the face of the whole earth.

— Genesis 11:4

A kind act by a stranger is a wonderful surprise! I don't expect someone to let me go ahead in line at the store or to return an item I had lost. What a blessing it is when people reach out to others. Thank you for the small acts that make my day better, and thank you for the opportunity to be a blessing to others by finding small ways to make their day brighter.

August 28

And thou shalt command the children of Israel, that they bring thee pure oil olive beaten for the light, to cause the lamp to burn always.

— Exodus 27:20

When I don't feel well, it is easy to feel sorry for myself. Then I remember the people who support me and help me when I am unwell. Thank you for the friends and family, the neighbors and coworkers, the nurses and doctors, and everyone else who goes out of the way to brighten my day and make me see a ray of light in the darkness.

August 29

Nevertheless we made our prayer unto our God, and set a watch against them day and night, because of them.

— *Nehemiah 4:9*

Lord, thank you for the gift of prayer. What an amazing gift it is to be able to speak to you any time I need to. May I remember to not only seek you in times of need, but to thank you for all the blessings in my life. May my time in prayer bring me closer to you and help me be grateful for all the wonderful things in my life.

August 30

And all the earth sought to Solomon, to hear his wisdom, which God had put in his heart.

— 1 Kings 10:24

Like a speed bump in the drive-through, a decision lies in our path, placed there by God to remind us hope is a choice. Choosing to live as people of hope is not to diminish or belittle pain and suffering or lie about evil's reality. Rather it is to cling to God's promise that he will make all things new.

August 31

What a gift friendship is! I am grateful for my friends. Some friends have known me for many years. We grew up together and watched each other change and grow. Other friends are newer, but no less dear. Thank you, Lord, for all the friends you have placed in my life and for the memories we have created together.

September

September 1

It's hard to be grateful for difficult times. Help me to
see my trials as an opportunity to grow and change.
Help me reach out to others who are suffering their
own difficult times. Thank you, God, for the chance
to know you better through my suffering. Help me
remember and be grateful for the suffering you endured
to help me. Let me find the bright side of every trial and
the strength to be grateful for the test.

September 2

Turn us again, O God, and cause thy face to shine; and
we shall be saved.

— Psalm 80:3

Thank you, Lord, for the inner light that shines within me. Help me to show that light to others and not hide it deep inside myself. Thank you for my talents and the things that I am good at. May I never forget how grateful I am to be able to share my abilities and bring joy to others.

September 3

For except we had lingered, surely now we had returned this second time.

— Genesis 43:10

Look at the clock. What time is it? Is it time to go? Are we running out of time? I need more time! Lord, help me to stop and relax and enjoy time instead of feeling like it is my enemy. Help me be grateful for each minute and the special joys it brings. Sometimes I need to slow down and think of time as my friend. Thank you, Lord, for time and the gifts it brings me.

September 4

Today I am thankful for my family. My parents, my siblings, my cousins and aunts and uncles…all are part of my family and my life. I may not be close to everyone or see everyone as often as I'd like, but I am grateful for their presence in my life. My family is a big part of who I am today. I need to thank them for that gift, even as I thank God for putting these special people in my life.

September 5

Every day is a journey through time and space. Thank you, Lord, for the journeys that make up my life and take me to amazing places. I am grateful for the things I've learned on my life's journey. Allow me to appreciate the journey more than the destination and keep an open mind for the unexpected gifts on the road. I may not always end up where I thought I would, but I am grateful for the paths I travel!

September 6

And she said, Let thine handmaid find grace in thy sight.
So the woman went her way, and did eat, and her countenance
was no more sad.

— 1 Samuel 1:18

I am thankful to the Lord for his gift of forgiveness. I know I am
not perfect and I know I make mistakes. Grant me the wisdom
and grace to know when I am wrong and to ask for forgiveness.
Give me a sense of gratitude toward those who forgive my errors,
and help me forgive others who have offended me.

September 7

I returned, and saw under the sun, that the race is not to the swift, nor the battle to the strong, neither yet bread to the wise, nor yet riches to men of understanding, nor yet favour to men of skill; but time and chance happeneth to them all.

— *Ecclesiastes 9:11*

Thank you, God, for second chances. Sometimes I feel like I can't do anything right. It's embarrassing to make mistakes. It's embarrassing to show others that I am less than perfect. Thank you for giving me the chance to try again, to make things right, and to improve myself. Help me find the courage to try again and show the world my best qualities!

September 8

Then Laban and Bethuel answered and said, The thing proceedeth from the Lord: we cannot speak unto thee bad or good.

— Genesis 24:50

Lord, sometimes I get frustrated, especially when I have to face something new. Thank you for giving me an open heart. Help me accept change and rejoice in new experiences and new people. Help me to be grateful for new opportunities and always see the good things even when I am afraid to try something new.

September 9

A good neighbor is a blessing! I am so grateful for the neighbors I have known and who have become my friends just by virtue of living close by. Together we have faced problems and shared memories. Thank you, Lord, for giving me good neighbors who will stand beside me and help make all our lives more complete.

September 10

Honour and majesty are before him: strength and beauty
are in his sanctuary.

— Psalm 96:6

God, help me notice the little things and be grateful for them.
All too often, we rush through life and don't notice the blessings
all around us. I am grateful for the chance to see beauty in the
smallest details. Help me remember to slow down and look. I am
grateful for the little bits of beauty scattered through my day

September 11

This is a sad and solemn day, yet there is still time to be thankful. Thank you, Lord, for all the emergency workers who help people every day. They bring light to the darkness and help to those who need it most. Thank you for their selflessness and willingness to give everything they have to save another. Just as Jesus sacrificed his life to save us, we are blessed by the sacrifices of those who save our lives.

September 12

And the Lord shall scatter you among the nations, and ye shall be left few in number among the heathen, whither the Lord shall lead you.

— Deuteronomy 4:27

Thank you for our leaders. I might not always agree with them, but it is good to have people who will take charge and lead us. Help me remember to be thankful for those who dedicate their lives to public service, and help me to appreciate their vision of a brighter future.

September 13

Behold, this is the joy of his way, and out of the earth shall others grow.

— Job 8:19

It's amazing how much joy an animal can bring into our lives. Today I am thankful for my pets—the ones I've had and the ones I know now. I am grateful for their love and companionship, and for somehow knowing when I need a hug or a cuddle. Sometimes it is good to just talk to animals and feel like they are really listening. Thank you, Lord, for the gift of animal companions.

September 14

Too often we hop in our cars or take the bus or train without thinking about how much these ways of transportation make our lives easier. I am grateful for transportation that helps me reach my destinations more quickly. How wonderful it is to get somewhere in just a few minutes or be able to visit someone who lives far away! With every bump of the wheels, may I be grateful for the machines that take me where I need to go.

September 15

And they cast lots, ward against ward, as well the small as the great,
the teacher as the scholar.

— *1 Chronicles 25:8*

Thank you, Lord, for teachers. How can I ever repay the men and women who taught me and opened my eyes to the world? How can I ever truly thank the people who teach my children and guide them on their journey through life? I am so grateful for those who teach and mentor. Thank you for giving us knowledge and wisdom to carry on life's path.

September 16

And thou shalt offer peace offerings, and shalt eat there, and rejoice before the Lord thy God.

— *Deuteronomy 27:7*

Today I am going to treat myself! Thank you for the opportunity to do something special "just because." Thank you for giving me the chance to reward myself just for being me. I am grateful for these little joys and for the ability to recognize that I am worthy of pampering. My life is special, and today I am thankful for the chance to rejoice in myself.

September 17

I wisdom dwell with prudence, and find out knowledge
of witty inventions.

— Proverbs 8:12

How different our lives would be without inventions! When I
think back to what life must have been like one hundred years
ago, I am grateful for the things that make my life easier. I
am glad to have machines to help me cook, clean, and stay
entertained. Thank you, God, for inspiring those who
came up the inventions that make my life so much
easier than my ancestors' lives.

September 18

Thank you for the gift of writing. What a joy it is to express myself through words! A letter, a diary entry, a blog, or a report…all these things are ways I can share my thoughts and knowledge with the world. I am grateful for the chance to express myself and pray that God will guide my pen every time I write.

September 19

Where would we be without our elders? When I think about the people who came before me, I am filled with gratitude for their hard work and sacrifices. It is good to remember what they did and how they lived. Thank you, Lord, for giving us strong forebears who shaped the world and always looked toward creating a better future. Without them, my life would be very different. Help me appreciate and value the past.

September 20

Thanks be unto God for his unspeakable gift.

— *2 Corinthians 9:15*

Today I will find a way to share my gifts with others. It might be something small, but I want to find a way to give something of myself. Thank you, Lord, for being able to share our gifts and for being givers. Even a small gift is a blessing, and I am grateful to both give and receive.

September 21

Till he fill thy mouth with laughing, and thy lips with rejoicing.

— Job 8:21

Today I am thankful for the gift of laughter. How wonderful it is to let out a big belly laugh and feel joy rush through my entire body! Thank you for the people who make me laugh, whether it is a neighbor or friend or a performer on television. Thank you for allowing me to experience joy bursting out of me, and help me make others feel happy with my laughter as well.

September 22

If we live in the Spirit, let us also walk in the Spirit.

— Galatians 5:25

Thank you, Lord, for the hobbies that I enjoy. How much joy I get out of these pleasures! Thank you for the chance to create, play, and enjoy. I am grateful for the people who share my hobby and who have become my friends. What a gift to share the joy of our pastimes together!

September 23

It is hard to be patient, but I am grateful for that gift. Whether it is waiting in line or anticipating a coming event, patience is a wonderful way to slow down and appreciate what is coming. Thank you for the gift of patience and the ability to take my time and savor every moment. Instead of saying, "I can't wait!" I am happy to say, "I will wait my turn" as I anticipate what is to come.

September 24

And the Lord gave the people favour in the sight of the Egyptians. Moreover the man Moses was very great in the land of Egypt, in the sight of Pharaoh's servants, and in the sight of the people.

— Exodus 11:3

Thank you, God, for my five senses. I am grateful for being able to see, hear, taste, touch, and smell. How wonderful to see nature's beauty, to hear the voices of my loved ones, to taste good food, to smell the fresh scent of spring, and to touch a loved one's skin. My senses let me experience the world, and I give thanks for that gift today.

September 25

Six days thou shalt work, but on the seventh day thou shalt rest: in earing time and in harvest thou shalt rest.

—Exodus 34:21

Thank you, Lord, at the harvest time. Thank you for the plants that grow to give us food and thank you for the people who grow them. The earth's bounty is a miracle! As I enjoy fresh food, may I always be grateful for what I eat and the nutrition it provides.

September 26

And Stephen, full of faith and power, did great wonders and miracles among the people.

— Acts 6:8

How beautiful is the work of your hands, Lord! I am grateful for the world of nature. How wonderful it is to see the plants and animals you have created. How awesome is your power on the shape of the earth! Thank you, Lord, for making the landscape and creating so much beauty in the natural world.

September 27

Sometimes it is so hard to take chances! Thank you, God, for giving me the courage to take a chance and try something new. I am so glad to be able to step out of my comfort zone and find the courage to change. What a gift to know that taking a chance could change my life! Thank you for the excitement of being brave.

September 28

For we through the Spirit wait for the hope of righteousness by faith.

— Galatians 5:5

I look around at work and think how wonderful it is that so many different people can become a team. Thank you, Lord, for my coworkers and supervisors. We may have our differences and our dark moments, but it is good to know that we are all working together toward a common goal. Thank you for the friendships I develop with my coworkers and for bringing us together in a special place.

September 29

Thank you for people who share their wisdom. Sometimes I may think I know everything, but it is good to realize that there are many people who are smarter than me. What a gift to receive their guidance in my life! Help me to have a listening ear and always be grateful for those who want to help me.

September 30

And thou say in thine heart, My power and the might of mine hand hath gotten me this wealth.

— Deuteronomy 8:17

Thank you, Lord, for the signs of your power. Thank you for the awe I feel during a thunderstorm or at the sight of a monument in nature. Thank you for the thrill I feel when I see one of your works in all its glory. It is good to know your power and feel its presence in my life.

October

October 1

Lord, I see you in the beauty of the autumn. Thank you for the brilliant colors of the trees. Thank you for the crisp, cool air that refreshes me. I am blessed to see autumn's beauty everywhere I go. Thank you for showing me that a time of change can be one of the most gorgeous seasons on Earth.

October 2

And Jesus said unto him, Verily I say unto thee, Today shalt thou be with me in paradise.

— Luke 23:43

Thank you, God, for my life. Today I realize I have so much to be thankful for. My life may not be perfect, but nevertheless it is full of good things, of beauty, and of many wonders. Thank you, Lord, for everything you have given me and the opportunities I've had. Pleasemake me aware of all I have to celebrate and be thankful for.

October 3

O love the Lord, all ye his saints: for the Lord preserveth the faithful, and plentifully rewardeth the proud doer.

— Psalm 31:23

Faith is a key that opens the door of abundance. Too many of us live behind locked doors of lack, suffering, and loneliness when everything we could possibly desire is on the other side, if only we turn the key. God has promised us abundant blessings, but first we must show him we have faith by moving towards the door without doubt, fear and uncertainty. Then, he will reveal a bounty of blessings to reward us.

October 4

And to rule over the day and over the night, and to divide the light from the darkness: and God saw that it was good.

— *Genesis 1:18*

I cannot see the light, but I know it is just up ahead. I cannot find the way out, but I know that my path is leading me there. I cannot solve the problem, but I know the solution is on its way. I know these things because of my faith in God, who has never failed me, and never will.

October 5

What does it mean to have faith? It means moving through the challenges of daily life with boldness because we know that someone has our back. It means approaching life's obstacles with courage and conviction because we know someone is looking out for us. It means walking with our heads held high because we know someone walks with us. That someone is God.

October 6

I may not know what the next step is, but God does. I may not understand why I am going through a particular challenge, but God does. The wisdom of God knows all and sees the bigger picture, when I am only able to grasp a small piece of the puzzle. I put my trust and faith in God's greater vision for my life and allow it to unfold according to his will.

October 7

If I say, I will forget my complaint, I will leave off my heaviness,
and comfort myself:
I am afraid of all my sorrows, I know that thou wilt not
hold me innocent.

— Job 9:27-28

Take comfort in God's steadfast presence.
Even when you suffer, take comfort
in the hope of God's healing.
Even when you fear, take comfort
in the hope of God's strength.
No matter what you face, take comfort
in knowing you never walk alone.

October 8

We all have days when nothing goes right, and all we want to do is crawl back to bed and curl up into a ball. Sometimes those days stretch into weeks and months of bleak depression. But God is always there, watching over us, gently urging us to have hope because he has a plan for us. We may not see it unfolding, but it is, and hope is the pathway there.

October 9

Shall thy lovingkindness be declared in the grave? or thy faithfulness in destruction?

— Psalm 88:11

To have hope is to put our life into the hands of a loving God that is always looking out for us, always making clear our path. When we are feeling down and about to give up, hope is like the sign on the road that tells us "rest stop ahead," and suddenly we feel renewed and refreshed, able to walk on just a bit longer and just a bit farther than we thought we could alone.

October 10

Make a joyful noise unto the Lord, all ye lands.

— Psalm 98:8

How joyful life becomes when we surrender to our faith in God, allowing his will to work through us. We give up resistance and frustration, and things suddenly seem to flow with greater ease. We still have obstacles, but also the strength and resources to overcome them. Living in faith and experiencing more peace and joy is what God intended for us!

October 11

To have faith is to have the promise of God's love to see you through any situation in life. Faith accompanies us, helping us to see the next step along the unseen path that is his will. When we step out of faith, we step away from the peace and comfort of God. Walking in faith is walking with God.

October 12

Let the saints be joyful in glory: let them sing aloud upon their beds.

— *Psalm 149:5*

When I can see no way out of the dark tunnel of despair, my faith becomes the bright beacon of light that guides my path. When I can feel no end to the pain I am suffering, my faith becomes the soothing balm that brings relief. My faith in God never disappoints me or abandons me. Even though I cannot see it, I know it is always at work in my life.

October 13

Therefore I went about to cause my heart to despair of all the labour which I took under the sun.

— *Ecclesiastes 2:20*

Lean on your faith when there is no one around to help. Like a strong pillar, faith in God can hold you up during the worst of storms and the harshest of winds. Faith gives you something to hold onto. Faith even brings you back home to God again when you are sure you are lost and alone.

October 14

Where there is no vision, the people perish: but he that keepeth
the law, happy is he.

— Proverbs 29:18

I may not know what the next step is, but God does. I may not
understand why I am going through a particular challenge, but
God does. The wisdom of God knows all and sees the bigger
picture, when I am only able to grasp a small piece of the puzzle.
I put my trust and faith in God's greater vision for my life and
allow it to unfold according to his will.

October 15

He shall fly away as a dream, and shall not be found: yea, he shall be chased away as a vision of the night.

— *Job 20:8*

What we cannot do for ourselves, God can do for us. With our limited vision and perception, only God's wisdom can look beyond our lack and limitations. How comforting is it to know that we have this resource to turn to anytime we need? God is always ready to help us, to advise us, and to direct us.

October 16

If I laughed on them, they believed it not; and the light of my countenance they cast not down.

— Job 29:24

When I am wrong, I turn within to find the right way. God's eternal wisdom is like a flowing river I can tap into at any time, especially when I am clueless and don't know which way to turn. I take comfort in knowing I don't have to be a genius and figure out every last detail of my life. God knows best, and as long as I stay in tune with his word, I will be divinely inspired.

October 17

This world is full of people who have to be right, even if it means losing friendships or family connections. The need to be right causes so much suffering. Instead, seek the need to be wise. Seek the ability to use your God-given wisdom to be of help to others, and not a burden. No one is right all the time, and it takes wisdom to realize that and to learn to be compassionate to others, and to yourself.

October 18

Do therefore according to thy wisdom, and let not his hoar head go down to the grave in peace.

— 1 Kings 2:6

What does the wisdom of God sound like? Like a soft whisper from within. What does the wisdom of God look like? Signs and miracles, big and small, that point to the answers to our problems. What does the wisdom of God feel like? Like a soft, comforting blanket on a cold day that wraps around us. It sounds, looks, and feels like love.

October 19

Friendships, like gardens, must be nourished and cultivated if they are to flourish and thrive. Take time to pull the weeds, turn the soil, and plant new seeds. Then enjoy the beauty of this love you have created

October 20

And they went in unto Noah into the ark, two and two of all flesh, wherein is the breath of life.

— *Genesis 7:15*

Intelligence is knowing with the mind. Wisdom is knowing with the heart. There are times in life when we must turn to the wisdom of our hearts for answers and direction, because the mind does not have that deeper knowing and understanding. Our hearts are the direct pipeline to God's loving wisdom, and only through the heart can we access it and put it to use in our lives.

October 21

An attitude of gratitude can help you get through even the roughest of times. Focusing on God's blessings helps you realize just how loved you are. It isn't about ignoring all the things that go wrong or bring you suffering, but always remembering to look for the blessing in the lesson, and the silver lining in the dark clouds above.

October 22

Now therefore, our God, we thank thee, and praise thy glorious name.

— 1 Chronicles 29:13

When I am thankful for what I have, I am given more. When I am not thankful, what I have is taken away. Gratitude is like a door that, when opened, leads to even more good things. But to be ungrateful keeps that door closed, and keeps me away from what God wants to bless me with. I am thankful, always.

October 23

What man of you, having an hundred sheep, if he lose one of them, doth not leave the ninety and nine in the wilderness, and go after that which is lost, until he find it?

— Luke 15:4

Even when you feel like you have nothing, the love of God remains. Being thankful for his presence will open your eyes to what you do have, and maybe never noticed before. God is always showering you with reasons to be thankful. Even when you feel like all is lost, God is there, and that alone is something to be grateful for.

October 24

And God called the light Day, and the darkness he called Night. And the evening and the morning were the first day.

— Genesis 1:5

Wake up in the morning and be grateful for the new day ahead. Every 24 hours is an opportunity to live life more fully, and love more deeply. Look at each moment and see the gift it brings. Cherish the present as it unfolds. Then, when you go to sleep at night, be thankful for the experiences God gave you. This is a life well-lived.

October 25

But seek ye first the kingdom of God, and his righteousness; and all these things shall be added unto you.

— Matthew 6:33

There is no denying the pleasure of creature comforts. Last year, my husband and I decided to take the plunge and have central air conditioning installed in our old home. Every hot day this past summer, I have reveled in returning to a blast of cool air when I get home; on some level, the air conditioning has made my life better. But as much as I appreciate it, I must remember not to be distracted by or consumed by physical comforts to the extent that I neglect my spiritual welfare.

Dear God, thank you for air conditioning—it is good to feel good! But may I always be cognizant of well-being on the inside as well as the outside; may my focus on the everlasting rewards of your kingdom be unswerving.

October 26

She is more precious than rubies: and all the things thou canst desire are not to be compared unto her.

— *Proverbs 3:15*

Life can be complicated; in the larger world we are challenged, sometimes on a daily basis, to be our best selves. Perhaps we don't see eye-to-eye with a coworker. Maybe we need to have a talk with a friend who has hurt us, even though we dislike confrontation. Can it be that the sweet, adoring toddler we walked to preschool seemingly yesterday has morphed into a teen who is trying to individuate—but doesn't yet know how to do that in a mature or loving way? Though life's hurts can chip away at our spirits, God reminds us that each of us has value. May we never lose sight of the fact that God created us! May we never lose sight of our inherent worth.

October 27

And blessed is she that believed: for there shall be a performance of those things which were told her from the Lord.

— *Luke 1:45*

Our relationships strengthen us. This came home to me the other day, when an exchange with a coworker left me feeling irresolute and unsettled. During my commute home, my stomach was in knots: I went over and over the disagreement in my head. It was hard to sort out whether I'd handled things with grace. When I got home, I found that my husband had started dinner; the warm atmosphere of love and regard unclenched my heart, and I was able to talk frankly about the day. My husband's nonjudgmental but clear-sighted perspective helped me sort how to remedy the situation; after we talked, we took a moment to pray together. God, thank you for reminding us of the importance of believing: in you, and in one another.

October 28

Have not I commanded thee? Be strong and of a good courage; be not afraid, neither be thou dismayed: for the Lord thy God is with thee whithersoever thou goest.

— *Joshua 1:9*

You can have those dreams you dream. God instilled them in you so you could express his love out into the world. Through your skills, talent, and creativity, God wants you to be epic! Make plans, and then let him work those plans through you in a miraculous way!

October 29

God has a mighty vision for my life, and I plan to live up to those expectations. Through the work I do, and the love I give, I hope to fulfill God's legacy of good in the world. I refuse to stay small when God is asking me to go big.

October 30

Today, in the dreary days as we head toward winter, I celebrate flowers. How wonderful it is to see their bright colors. I am grateful for the chance to bring flowers into my home to brighten a dreary day. Thank you for the colors and smells of spring and the opportunity to welcome them into my life at any time of year.

October 31

Happy Halloween! Even though Halloween is built around fear, it can also be a time of joy and gratitude. Thank you for the joy I feel when I see children dressed in costume and enjoying their special night. Thank you for a day when everyone can be as weird as they want to be. Thank you for letting us celebrate the unusual and see the world in a different way.

November

November 1

Dear God, I long to change parts of my life that are no longer working, but don't know where to start. Help me break down these big, scary goals into small and achievable steps. Give me courage to put these plans into action and turn my life around!

November 2

Lift up thyself, thou judge of the earth: render a reward to the proud.

— Psalm 94:2

In the planning stages of a goal, it's hard to stay committed. There are so many distractions that steal our time and attention. But if we hold on for the long haul, our plans turn into achievements we can truly be proud of.

November 3

But if the cloud were not taken up, then they journeyed not till the day that it was taken up.

— Exodus 40:37

Whenever I make plans for anything in my life, I check with God in prayer first. If it rings true in my heart, which is where God speaks to me, I go for it. The ideas may be mine, but the inspiration and motivation to make them a reality come from God.

November 4

By the great force of my disease is my garment changed: it bindeth me about as the collar of my coat.

— Job 30:18

Father God, watch over me as I begin this new journey. I made my plans and created a blueprint for change. I now ask your help carrying it out in the world. Guide me along and help me adjust my path when my plans don't always pan out the way I hoped. Amen.

November 5

And we dreamed a dream in one night, I and he; we dreamed each man according to the interpretation of his dream..

— *Genesis 41:11*

I know with God on my side, I cannot fail. The joyful plans I make for my goals and dreams are infused with his love and grace. All I do is listen for his voice within and I am on my way to a bold, new me!

November 6

We will know when it's time to make our stand. God will speak to us a little louder, a little stronger. The whisper within will become a mighty roar, as we are encouraged to step out in faith and be who God meant us to be.

November 7

He will not regard any ransom; neither will he rest content, though thou givest many gifts.

— Proverbs 6:35

You may be afraid, but you've got the power of God on your side. So stand up and be the fullest and deepest expression of yourself you can possibly be. Let God do his will in your life and light up the world with your brilliance, your talents, and the gifts only you can give!

November 8

How that in a great trial of affliction the abundance of their joy and their deep poverty abounded unto the riches of their liberality.

— *2 Corinthians 8:2*

God, I ask for a bold and courageous faith to get me through these trials and tribulations. Let me stand on my own feet, but steady my footing with the knowledge of your presence. Give me the strength of will to never give up, no matter how crazy life gets.

November 9

Be of the same mind one toward another. Mind not high things, but condescend to men of low estate. Be not wise in your own conceits.

— *Romans 12:16*

When the world rocks you off your center, hold fast to God to bring you back to harmony and balance. When life pulls the rug out from under you, jump and land square on the foundation of God's love for you. When all seems lost, God will help you find your way again.

November 10

I may not understand your ways, God, or what your plans are for me, but I trust you. I know you have my best interest always at heart, and you won't lead me astray. My trust in your will acts like a lighthouse beacon guiding me safely to shore.

November 11

Thank you for our veterans and those who serve in the military. May I always remember those who have given up their day-to-day lives just to keep me and my country safe and secure. Help me to show my gratitude toward the veterans I meet and always remember to honor their sacrifices.

November 12

And he stayed yet other seven days; and sent forth the dove; which returned not again unto him any more.

— *Genesis 8:12*

Dear God, I could use a steadying hand today. My life seems like a roller coaster, filled with so many ups and downs it's making my head spin. I could use a fortifying courage today. I'm being dealt so many lousy cards to play. Help me keep the faith, God, and stay in your will for me. Amen.

November 13

Intreat the Lord (for it is enough) that there be no more mighty thunderings and hail; and I will let you go, and ye shall stay no longer.

— *Exodus 9:28*

God, when I feel unsteady, you alone provide the firm ground beneath my feet. Illuminate my path so that I am always living in your will and not from my own limited ego. Show me how to be the best I can be under all circumstances, good and bad.

November 14

And I will make thee exceeding fruitful, and I will make nations of thee, and kings shall come out of thee.

— *Genesis 17:6*

If you want your dreams to bear big fruit, you must be patient enough to let the buds grow into fullness, even if it feels like it's taking forever. Remember, God's timing is not your timing. Stick to it! Don't give up just before you get that bold breakthrough!

November 15

And the earth was without form, and void; and darkness was upon the face of the deep. And the Spirit of God moved upon the face of the waters.

— Genesis 1:2

Having faith in God is important, but even he expects us to move our feet. Without taking action, his words of wisdom go unheeded, and his will goes unfulfilled. We best serve ourselves when we listen for his word, then move forward boldly.

November 16

Dear God,
When obstacles threaten to derail me from the path
towards my goals, give me the strength to go forward
anyway, even if it means taking a little detour. Help me
keep my pace, and not become weak of body or spirit over
the long road ahead.

November 17

And it came to pass after this, that Joash was minded to repair the house of the Lord.

— 2 Chronicles 24:4

God, the knowledge that your promises will be fulfilled keeps me going through the toughest of days and nights. I know if I stay strong and power through, I will be richly rewarded in body, mind, and spirit.

November 18

And Elijah said unto Elisha, Tarry here, I pray thee; for the Lord hath sent me to Bethel. And Elisha said unto him, As the Lord liveth, and as thy soul liveth, I will not leave thee. So they went down to Bethel.

— 2 Kings 2:2

God gives us strength to go with our friends and share their burdens and responsibilities. When my friend and mentor, Diane, needed to travel to a cancer clinic in another city, I felt called to accompany her. I could not change her diagnosis, but I could be there, as a friend and companion, as she has been there for me these many years.

Dear God, thank you for the powerful gift of friendship. May I tap into your strength to be steadfast and true to my friends; as Elisha accompanied Elijah, may I walk beside my friends in good times and bad.

November 19

Now when Job's three friends heard of all this evil that was come upon him, they came every one from his own place; Eliphaz the Temanite, and Bildad the Shuhite, and Zophar the Naamathite: for they had made an appointment together to come to mourn with him and to comfort him.

— *Job 2:11*

God puts friends in our lives to comfort us, support us, and share our burdens during dark times. And groups of friends can be powerful, indeed: Carrie, a single mom of two who lost her consulting job during an economic downturn, still remembers the solace provided by the prayer circle at her community church as she interviewed for a new position. "I knew others were thinking of me and praying for me," she shares.
"It gave me strength."

Dear Lord, in lonely and discouraging times, may I never lose sight of the people you have put in my life. May I always remember the power of loving kindness, multiplied!

November 20

To every thing there is a season, and a time to every
purpose under the heaven.

— Ecclesiastes 3:1

You don't need to run a marathon. Just take one step at a time.
Go out in faith and let God guide you. There is a season for
everything, and God has perfect timing. Just listen and when he
tells you to move, move!

November 21

So teach us to number our days, that we may apply
our hearts unto wisdom.

— Psalm 90:12

I watch the days of my life fly by, always thinking of what I need
to do tomorrow, next week, next month. God, help me to slow
down and take it all one step at a time, and drink in every present
moment, for these moments will never come again.

November 22

Then said Samuel to the people, Come, and let us go to Gilgal, and renew the kingdom there.

— *1 Samuel 11:14*

How much happier and at peace would we be if we allowed God to order our days? If we just focus on the promises of his love for us, all else will fall into place accordingly, without our exhausting effort.

November 23

*The meek will he guide in judgment: and the meek
will he teach his way.*

— *Psalm 25:9*

Guidance is there, but you must look with your heart. Let go of
what the mind and ego see, for it is not the truth. Follow where
your heart leads, for it is led by the spirit of a loving and powerful
God who wants what is best for you!

November 24

O Lord, as we enter this season of thanksgiving, how
important it is for us to grasp the concept of "enough."
You know how this world tempts us with all that is bigger,
better—more in every way! But there is such joy and
freedom in trusting that you will give us exactly what
we need—neither too little nor too much. May we never
take for granted all the blessings we have, Lord,
and may we be as generous with others as you are with
us. It is the simple life that brings us closest to you; we are
blessed when we live simply.

November 25

Be not overcome of evil, but overcome evil with good.

— *Romans 12:21*

God, teach me to have the courage to act in the world as you wish me to. Help me find a way to push through the challenges that arise in my path, and show me how to overcome evil with love and compassion. Help me to stand tall against fear and stay in the light. Amen.

November 26

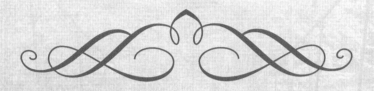

Dear God,
I ask today for a bold new vision for my life. I ask for the
strength and wisdom to be a better person to all those I
come in contact with. I ask for the courage to step out of
my comfort zone and expand my capacity for joy.

November 27

Take the choice of the flock, and burn also the bones under it, and
make it boil well, and let them seethe the bones of it therein.

— Ezekiel 24:5

It seems so insignificant,
this choice you have to make.
Yet the Lord can use small acts of faith
to cause the earth to shake!
So pray and wait to know his will
for decisions made today,
and the Lord may use your faithfulness
to show someone the way.

November 28

And the Lord said unto Moses, Pharaoh's heart is hardened, he refuseth to let the people go.

— Exodus 7:14

The wisdom and insight we need is often hidden in plain sight, right before our eyes, and under our very noses. God is always guiding us, if we stop and open our hearts and spirits to the still, small whisperings within that point the way.

November 29

We don't really know why we have to get sick, Lord. We only know your promise: No matter where we are or what we are called to endure, there you are in the midst of it with us, never leaving our side. Not for a split second. Thank you, Lord of all.

November 30

But my God shall supply all your need according to his riches in glory by Christ Jesus.

— Philippians 4:19

God is bigger than any problem you have. Whoever is opposing you is a weakling compared to God. Why not tap into God's supply of strength? Why focus on your problem when God is so much more interesting?

December

December 1

Sometimes it is difficult to appreciate snowy weather, but I thank God for the gift of snow days. How wonderful it is for everyone to be home, safe and warm. On snow days, life returns to a simpler pace and the demands of schedules and responsibilities fall away. Thank you, Lord, for the beauty of the snow and the time it gives us to relax and share quiet times with our loved ones.

December 2

And thou shalt love the Lord thy God with all thine heart, and with all thy soul, and with all thy might.

— *Deuteronomy 6:5*

Like the weather, love has its change of seasons. It begins with the springtime of courtship, merging into the sweet summer of devotion. When autumn arrives, so, too, do the rewards of commitment and sharing. Winter often brings a sense of comfort and contentment, but just as the weather is cyclical, so, too, is love. Just beyond winter is an even brighter spring of renewed passion, internal beauty, and deeper devotion.

December 3

But as they sailed he fell asleep: and there came down a storm of wind on the lake; and they were filled with water, and were in jeopardy.

— Luke 8:23

All around, the storms may churn,
the seas may rage, the fires burn.
But deep within you, you will not fear,
you will have peace when centered there.
For even amidst the tempest wild,
God will be there to guide you, child.

December 4

Now therefore, O king, come down according to all the desire of thy soul to come down; and our part shall be to deliver him into the king's hand.

— *1 Samuel 23:20*

We do not naturally love like God does, but we can desire to grow in demonstrating his love to others. Our Christian fervor can be measured by our desire to grow in love, in spite of the struggles we will undoubtedly encounter.

December 5

MY AIM IS...

to please him through communing in prayer

to show his love and for others care

to read his word as my guide for life

to cease my grumbling that causes strife

to be open to God's leading and his will

to take time to meditate, be quiet, and still

to continually grow in my Christlike walk

to be more like Jesus in my life and my talk.

December 6

There is no fear in love; but perfect love casteth out fear: because fear hath torment. He that feareth is not made perfect in love.

— 1 John 4:18

We respond to stresses in our lives with either fear or faith. Fear is a great threat to our faith. That's why we read often in the scriptures the directive, "Fear not." The closer we draw to God, the more our fears diminish.

December 7

God, I know you're not in a hurry—
your plans for me are on time.
You need no schedule or reminders
for I'm always on your mind.

I know you have drawn the mosaic
and you're fitting each tile in place.
As I continue to follow your plan,
help me not to hurry or race.

Waiting is so often difficult,
and patience I don't easily learn.
But to have my life more Christ-like
is for what I seek and yearn.

So as my life's pattern continues
and the next part begins to unfold,
it's you I'm trusting and praising,
it's your hand I cling to and hold.

December 8

When we think of integrity, we think of someone who is honorable and trustworthy — a person who keeps their word and guards their reputation. To be called a man or woman of integrity is a high compliment. Such a person knows the difference between right and wrong and diligently pursues doing right, no matter what the obstacles. Jesus provides the best example of a man of integrity; he was not swayed by outer influences but lived a life above reproach. Integrity comes not just from the pursuit of right living, but the pursuit of God, which leads to right living.

December 9

These things I have spoken unto you, that in me ye might have peace.
In the world ye shall have tribulation: but be of good cheer; I have
overcome the world.

— John 16:33

Sometimes we believe our souls can only be at peace if there is no
outer turmoil. The wonder of God's peace is that even when the
world around us is in confusion and our emotions are in a whirl,
underneath it all we can know his peace.

December 10

And the man wondering at her held his peace, to wit whether the Lord had made his journey prosperous or not.

— Genesis 24:21

Peace is about releasing.
It's about opening my hand
and letting go of my plan,
my agenda,
my demands
on God and other people
and even on myself.
It's about realizing
that every person
is as important as I am
in God's eyes.
It's remembering
I don't know everything
and I don't have solutions
to every problem.
It's about calling on
the One who does.

December 11

Then hear thou in heaven their prayer and their supplication, and maintain their cause.

— 1 Kings 8:45

People can often sense when someone is in need of prayer— even if that someone is miles away. If the thought of a friend should come into your mind, why not stop and say a little prayer on their behalf?

December 12

And they fell upon their faces, and said, O God, the God of
the spirits of all flesh, shall one man sin, and wilt thou be wroth
with all the congregation?

— *Numbers 16:22*

Being a friend means that you need to reach out. Is there
someone you can think of who needs to know that you are there
for them—that you are a friend who cares? Pray for the spirit
of friendship to so light up your life that you'll radiate this
brightness to someone who needs you.

December 13

When we think of joy, we often think of things that are new—a new day, a new baby, a new love, a new beginning, the promise of a new home with God in heaven. Rejoicing in these things originates with having joy in the God who makes all things new. Rather than relying on earthly pleasures to provide happiness, the Scriptures command that we rejoice in God and in each new day he brings. Joy is a celebration of the heart that goes beyond circumstances to the very foundation of joy—the knowledge that we are loved by God.

December 14

And all the people came up after him, and the people piped
with pipes, and rejoiced with great joy, so that the earth rent
with the sound of them.

—1 Kings 1:40

We all want to be happy, but joy goes much deeper. Joy is not
based on circumstances or feelings, which change like the
weather. True joy comes from a celebration of the heart over the
things that do not change—things that come from God.

December 15

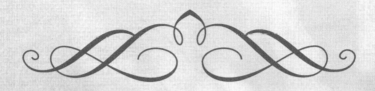

God of my heart, I am a broken person. I do not know how to handle this suffering. I am not strong enough to do it alone. Be my strength, God, and do for me what I simply cannot do for myself. Be the glue that binds the pieces of my shattered soul back together, that I may rise and step back onto the joyful path of life again. Amen.

December 16

Blessed be the God and Father of our Lord Jesus Christ, who hath blessed us with all spiritual blessings in heavenly places in Christ.

— Ephesians 1:3

Lift up your heart in sweet surrender to the God who is waiting to shower you with blessings. Lift up your soul on wings of joy to the God who is waiting to guide you from the chaos of shadows out into the light of a peace that knows no equal.

December 17

Regard not them that have familiar spirits, neither seek after wizurds,
to be defiled by them: I am the Lord your God.

— Leviticus 19:13

God, make me an open vessel through which the waters of your
spirit flow freely. Let your love move through me and out into my
world, touching everyone I come in contact with. Express your joy
through the special talents you have given me, that others may
come to know your presence in their own lives by witnessing your
presence in mine. Amen.

December 18

I have seen his ways, and will heal him: I will lead him also, and restore comforts unto him and to his mourners.

— Isaiah 57:18

When someone breaks our heart, we mourn, we grieve, and we feel the pain of rejection. We pray to God for healing and relief. And then we pick up the pieces and, with God's help and guidance, rebuild a heart that is even stronger, more resilient, and ready to love again.

December 19

Then spake Jesus again unto them, saying, I am the light of the world: he that followeth me shall not walk in darkness, but shall have the light of life.

— John 8:12

The God who hung the stars in space will turn
    your darkness into light.
The God whose birds rise on the winds will give
    your injured soul new flight.
The God who taught the whale its song will
    cause your heart to sing again.
For the God whose power made Earth and sky
    will touch you with his gentle hand.

December 20

Thou shalt therefore sacrifice the passover unto the Lord thy God, of the flock and the herd, in the place which the Lord shall choose to place his name there.

— Deuteronomy 16:2

This is not a choice I would make, for me or for the one who went against my standards, my hopes. It's a riddle, O God, why you give us freedom to choose. It can break our hearts. Comfort me as I cope with a choice not mine; forgive any role I had in it. Help me separate doer from deed as I pass on your words to all: "...nothing can separate us." Not even poor choices I sometimes make myself.

December 21

Tangled in tape, lists, and holiday wrappings, we are all thumbs of excitement! Bless the surprises we've selected, wrapped, and hidden. Restore us to the joy of anticipation. We want to be surprised, too. Our wish lists include the gift of peace possibilities, of ears to hear a summons and eyes to spot another's need or triumph, of being able to make a difference. As we cut and tape, God of surprises, remind us to keep in touch with the gift's recipient after the wrapping papers are long gone and the ornaments packed.

December 22

Shopping, wrapping, traveling, cooking. So much to do this season as we hurry toward the manger, answering God's call as did those folks so long ago, to go, believe, and do. Practice the notes of the carol, for soon it will be time to sing out "Gloria!" at what we'll see and hear.

December 23

And knew her not till she had brought forth her firstborn son: and he called his name Jesus.

— Matthew 1:25

Jesus, small poor baby of Bethlehem,

be born again in our hearts today

be born again in our homes today

be born again in our congregations today

be born again in our neighborhoods today

be born again in our cities today

be born again in our nations today

be born again in our world today.

December 24

Compassionate and holy God, we celebrate your coming into this world. We celebrate with hope, we celebrate with peace, we celebrate with joy. Through your giving our lives are secure. Through your love we, too, can give love. You are the source of our being. Joy to our world.

December 25

Merry Christmas! Thank you, Lord, for this special day. It is the birthday of your son, Jesus, and a bright and beautiful day for the world. Today I am grateful for rebirth, for celebrations, for sharing traditions with the people I love. Thank you for the gift of joy and new life.

December 26

For the word of God is quick, and powerful, and sharper than any twoedged sword, piercing even to the dividing asunder of soul and spirit, and of the joints and marrow, and is a discerner of the thoughts and intents of the heart.

— Hebrews 4:12

For just as the harshest winter always gives way to the warm blush of spring, the season of our suffering will give way to a brighter tomorrow, where change becomes a catalyst for new growth and spiritual maturity, and we are able to move on with the joyfulness of being alive.

December 27

The sting of rejection lingers long after it has been inflicted. It often creates an aversion to drawing near to the very thing that can bring healing: love through a relationship with God. It takes a certain willingness to risk reaching out to be forgiven by God if we ever hope to find wholeness again. But there is no more worthwhile risk than that which risks for the sake of God's love.

December 28

And the Lord God said, It is not good that the man should be alone; I will make him an help meet for him.

— Genesis 2:18

I blew it. Again. O Lord, help me know that wringing my hands in the wake of failure is as useless as lamenting storm-felled trees. Give me eyes to see beyond chaos to possibilities. In that way, I won't miss finding out what could happen if I picked up a saw and took to that tree, making firewood around which friends can gather.

December 29

And in process of time it came to pass, that Cain brought of the fruit of the ground an offering unto the Lord.

— Genesis 4:3

We become discouraged when we try to live according to our own time clocks. We want what we want, and we want it this very minute. Then, when we don't get it, we sink in the quicksand of hopelessness and defeat. Only when we realize that God is at work in our lives will we begin to relax and let things happen in due season. Fruit will not ripen any faster because we demand it but will ripen in all its sweet splendor when it is ready in spite of our demands.

December 30

For the kingdom of God is not in word, but in power.

— *1 Corinthians 4:20*

The creative power within is your power to overcome any
   obstacle and break through any binding walls that keep you
from your dreams. This power was given to you by the greatest
   of all creators, the One who created you, God. Just look around
at the amazing beauty and diversity of the world you live in,
and you will never again doubt that God supports your
   creative endeavors.

December 31

But they that wait upon the Lord shall renew their strength; they shall mount up with wings as eagles; they shall run, and not be weary; and they shall walk, and not faint.

— *Isaiah 40:31*

The slate is clean, Lord, the calendar as bare as the Christmas tree. Bless the New Year that beckons. We sing of you as help in ages past but need to know you as hope for years to come. Help us face what we must, celebrate every triumph we can, and make any changes we need. We're celebrating to the fullest this whistle-blowing, toast-raising moment, for it is the threshold between the old and new in us.